contents

MANIFESTO

Every day we are issued with new directives from those who are trying to run our lives: how many bits of fruit and vegetables we should eat; the exact amount of exercise we have to take to avoid obesity; how many units of alcohol we should imbibe or risk being considered a binger. Has government ever been more intrusive? Is there a single aspect of our lives not monitored by the do-gooders and the thought police? Go for a walk and you'll see yellow signs by rivers warning you of 'Danger – water'. Stand by a historic building and you're bound to see the notice 'Danger of falling masonry'. Go to the library or a post office and you'll be confronted with government leaflets (printed at our expense) telling us to eat all our food, hang our clothes out to dry if the weather is good and take a shower instead of a bath. Talk about stating the bloody obvious! Simple things we used to enjoy – bonfires, fireworks, the village tug-of-war or a children's party – now get cancelled because no one can afford to pay the insurance policies demanded by Health and Safety experts. How did we ever manage before the thought police and the nanny state took over? Some days I feel as if I am living in a climate of fear: full of anxiety about the state of the planet, worries about not saving money, and a deep-seated sense of guilt that I am failing to live up to impossible standards. I'm meant to be counting calories, cutting waste, off-setting my carbon, recycling everything but the kitchen sink, growing vegetables, make-do-and-mending my clothes, meanwhile not forgetting to eat five fruit and veg a day and drink no more than two units of alcohol whilst fitting in a thirty-minute walk.

So how to keep our sanity when we are pushed about by forces determined to drive us round the bend, who might rip us off and spit us out, confused, broke and frustrated at the end of it? From banks to insurance companies, credit card companies to mortgage lenders, we are bombarded with paperwork, mindless officialdom, incomprehensible jargon and baffling rules and regulations. At the same time our government wants to snoop on our emails and phone calls, have access to our personal data, and is determined we will carry ID cards, even though we've said time and time again we don't see the need for them.

I make a good Soup!

Says 'POTATO PETE'

On top of all that, grim news about the recession is beamed at us daily. Disposable income has plummeted to the lowest level for years, and we have less to spend on food, booze, holidays and clothes. Living standards are predicted to continue to drop, as jobs are cut and factories placed on short time or enforced breaks. Most of us are facing this trying time ill-equipped, burdened with debt, our earnings eaten up by large mortgages and fuel and household bills.

So, things are tough enough financially, but at the same time we're also relentlessly nagged by the do-gooders. Politicians have become nursemaids, moaning on about our health. The Green Lobby beseeches us to consume less, respect the environment more, conserve energy and increase the amount we recycle. There are myriad decisions to be taken every day. Do we buy cheap clothes from the Third World, where working conditions may be unacceptable? Do we buy vegetables that have been flown halfway round the world, or let peasant farmers in Africa go bust as we cut down on our air miles? Do we buy local vegetables if they are not organic? Do we patronise farmers' markets if they

seem expensive and only open on the weekend? Is it a guilty secret to do most of your shopping at the nearest supermarket because it's more convenient? The list seems endless. We are snowed under by conflicting advice and competing lobby groups. Some want to save the planet and urge us to consume less – the government wants us to spend more in order to kick-start the economy and save manufacturing and retail jobs. It's enough to drive you round the f***ing bend.

As if this weren't enough, we work longer hours and spend a large amount of time travelling, so we increasingly enlist helpers from childminders to cleaners to manage the homes we hardly spend any time in. And how do you find a builder or a handyman when the one you live with is too knackered to do more than slump in front of the telly? Even worse, one-fifth of all young men have no idea how to wire a plug, a third can't unblock a sink, and even more have no idea how to paint a wall. How to cope? How to get your life back and have some fun? Well, there's no point in letting it get to you. This book is your guide to keeping your spirits up, cutting through the crap and deciding which rules you're going to live your life by, on your terms. To achieve your goal of smiling through a credit crisis and not looking like a bag person from the Third World, it's time to get a grip.

Take a deep breath, decide what you won't bother doing any more and substitute activities that give you pleasure and make your limited resources go further. The first thing to do is strip the excess out of your life, get rid of the dead wood, the unnecessary things that drain your energy and waste your time. It's time to come up with a list of what you never need to buy again. Look at your relationships and acquaintances – decide who is superfluous. Dump the people in your life who are takers and exude negative energy, sign up with the neighbours and friends who are positive, can-do people. Realise that pooling your resources with others in the community makes them go further. Equip yourself with a few simple ground rules to cut through officialdom, deal with irritating call centres and pompous sales operatives and get the results you, not they, need.

this is dress I thought you'd look nice in!

Life is a journey and we're experiencing a bumpy patch – but there's no reason why you shouldn't emerge from it a great deal happier.

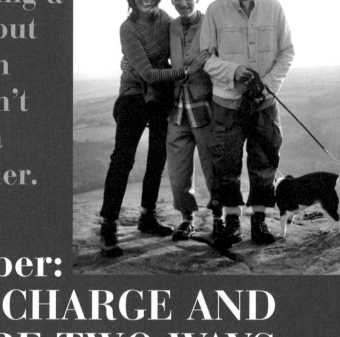

Just remember: YOU'RE IN CHARGE AND THERE ARE TWO WAYS TO GET THROUGH LIFE: YOUR WAY AND THE WRONG WAY.

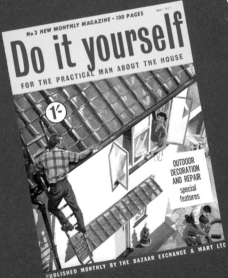

MUMBO JUMBO

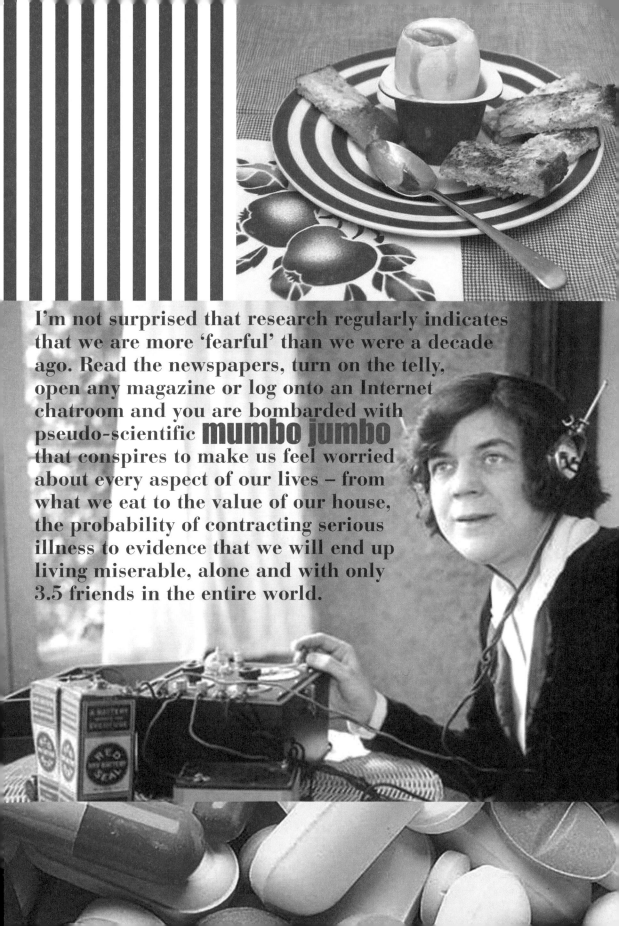

I'm not surprised that research regularly indicates that we are more 'fearful' than we were a decade ago. Read the newspapers, turn on the telly, open any magazine or log onto an Internet chatroom and you are bombarded with pseudo-scientific **mumbo jumbo** that conspires to make us feel worried about every aspect of our lives – from what we eat to the value of our house, the probability of contracting serious illness to evidence that we will end up living miserable, alone and with only 3.5 friends in the entire world.

One of the biggest problems about living in an age where information is spewed out every moment of the day is that so much of it turns out, on close inspection, to be either blatantly untrue, derived from biased research, or **so trivial it's not worth bothering about.** Increasingly, governments have decided to adopt the role of nanny/nag and drip-feed us depressing statistics about how we are eating and drinking ourselves to an early grave.

Once we elected politicians to run the country on our behalf so we could get on with our lives – now they've decided to replace mum and dad from afar and the country is going bankrupt

while they agonise about how to get us eating five portions of fruit and veg a day ... no wonder we're anxious. It's enough to make you reach for a bag of crisps and a glass of wine and vow not to vote in the next election.

Our parent's generation had a bath once a week, coped with epidemics of polio and diphtheria, had to survive on rationing, rarely ate meat and heated their homes with tiny coal fires or one bar electric heaters used *extremely sparingly*. Their cities were full of smog, holidays were taken in freezing Blighty and foreign travel non-existent.

Look at how healthy and thin everyone looked back in 1960! Today, it's a badge of honour for any minor league celebrity or second-division model to claim to be 'allergic' to something, and scientists struggle to understand why more children have asthma than ever before. **I cannot claim to have any allergies, except one – a profound distrust of any news story that starts 'Scientists have discovered...'.**

I grew up eating sugar, drinking milk in my tea, eating white bread and fried eggs. What a bloody miracle I have survived to 60 plus without allergies to wheat, dairy or animal fats, without a backside the size of a bus. I coped with catching nits, being hospitalised for amoebic dysentery (generally caught through eating salads contaminated with human or animal faeces), being hit by a motorbike, and falling on an iron stake in the park. (No it did not pass through my heart, before you write and ask!)

THE GREAT EGG SCANDAL

For years we were told that eating too many eggs would cause heart attacks. Mind you, back in the 1960s we ate (on average) five a week, with no ill effects. Poultry farmers complained in 1971 as sales of eggs plummeted when the British Heart Foundation ordered us to eat no more than three or four a week because eggs contained cholesterol which (they said) could increase the chance of a heart attack if high levels were present in the blood. Then in 1988 government minister Edwina Currie dealt the humble egg another blow, by claiming that most were infected with salmonella. In 2005 the BHF revised their guidelines and said eggs were OK, but by then the damage had been done and most of us thought that eating too many eggs was harmful. By 2009, however, nutritionists were begging people to eat eggs, claiming there was NO link between normal egg consumption and heart disease. Their new guidelines say it's more important to cut down on saturated fats found in dairy products, fatty meats, biscuits and cakes. By 2009, the BHF was telling us, 'We recommend that eggs can be eaten as part of a balanced diet'.
EXACTLY!

MUMBO JUMBO

15

DETOX DRIVEL

Somebody's going to need **Alka-Seltzer** for Indigestion!

Indigestion caused by unwise eating is quickly relieved by one or two Alka-Seltzer tablets dissolved in cold or warm water. Speedy Alka-Seltzer neutralizes excess stomach acid, and brings quick relief from discomfort as millions of people have found.

There's nothing quite like Alka-Seltzer for Indigestion and Headaches

Back in the 1980s, we didn't have toxins. We ate and drank too much, got hangovers and felt a bit flabby. **So we drank water, ate less for a week, had a couple of nights in, went to bed early and within a couple of days generally felt better.** The trouble with that old-fashioned, cheap regime is that it doesn't leave any scope for products (other than painkillers and Alka-Seltzer) to be flogged to us, the naïve punter. The concept of toxins was invented relatively recently by the alternative health industry to pander to our vanity, by implying that we can purge our bodies of unwelcome intruders and we will be purer and more beautiful as a result. Since the 1990s, celebrity nutritionists like Gillian McKeith have built their whole careers around warning us about these highly dangerous things called

that have to be eliminated at all cost. TV personalities like Carol Vorderman made a mint out of championing their special detox diets, available on DVDs, in books and printed in every women's magazine. The **so-called experts** then branched out into detox foods – making them even more money in the process. This whole dubious business is based on the spurious concept that toxins build up in our blood and may eventually damage our health. This debatable theory belittles the thousands of mine and factory workers fighting for compensation all over the world who really do suffer from blood poisoning and a range of serious illnesses caused by pollutants, which have been absorbed into their bodies and have damaged their well-being over a number of years.

Drink this much Florida Orange Juice every day!

A FULL BIG GLASS

Whee — it's Vitamin "C"!

There's a big difference between being poisoned by drinking too much red wine and suffering lung damage from working in a chemical factory. But when you read the rubbish written about toxins on the health and beauty pages of women's magazines you'd think that unless you are willing to remove them from your body, you're more or less asking for a shorter life.

MAKES CHILDREN AND ADULTS AS FAT AS PIGS.

No CURE NO PAY

Price 50 Cents

GROVE'S TASTELESS CHILL TONIC

ON THE MARKET OVER 20 YEARS
1½ MILLION BOTTLES SOLD LAST YEAR

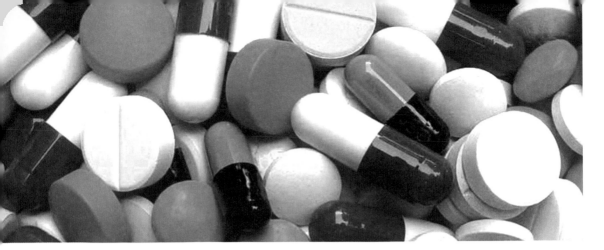

The British Dietetic Association (BDA), which represents over 6000 dieticians in the UK, has stated categorically that **there is no lotion or potion that will magically remove chemicals from the body.** Detox diets generally tell people to cut out certain food groups, which almost always include alcohol, meat, caffeine, processed foods, wheat and refined sugars. **You are told to drink gallons of water to 'flush' out the offending toxins. Dozens of drinks and pills are on sale containing minerals and vitamins that they claim help the 'cleansing' process.**

The trouble is, that's too simple for the mumbo jumbo toxin queens.

The BDA says the body is perfectly capable of removing its own waste without any extra help from these products, and a better way of feeling fitter would be to drink around eight glasses of water a day, plan meals ahead to avoid snacking, and eat one extra portion of fruit or vegetables a day.

HEART ATTACK BOLLOCKS

I don't know why I haven't dropped down dead from a heart attack. I lose my temper, I like everything neat and tidy, and I believe there are two ways to do everything – my way and the wrong way. The fact is, heart attacks are caused by a combination of genetics and lifestyle – and don't believe anything else.

Eat normally, walk 30 minutes a day, try to achieve the target weight for your height, and that's about it. But read and believe the mumbo jumbo written about heart attacks and you're quite likely to bring one on anyway.
According to one lot of scientists, fasting for 24 hours could cut your risk of coronary artery disease by 'up to 40%'. But when you discover that the people who took part in the survey were largely Mormons in Salt Lake City, Utah (who fast once a month as part of their religion), you're a lot less likely to take the findings seriously. Another survey in Denmark (but widely publicised in the UK press) found that *moderate drinkers who exercised were 50% less likely to suffer from heart disease than teetotallers.* So, up to fourteen units of alcohol a week combined with walking is good for the heart. Exactly what I've been practising for decades!

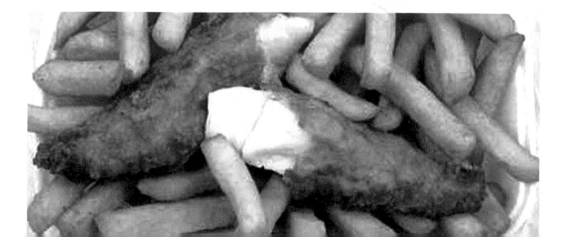

DEMON DRINK – THE UNIT MYTH – and WHY FAT-BUSTER IDEAS FAIL

I don't know why government bangs on about the recommended daily number of units (RDU) for men and women, as no one I know has ever answered any question about their drinking habits truthfully, unless they've been through rehab and given booze up for good. *It has always seemed ludicrous to me that men are allowed more than women – why? Is this not just another example of a male conspiracy at work? (After all, most government officials are men, most cabinet ministers are men, and the people running the NHS tend to have a willy.)* **What about tall, thin women versus weedy blokes? Shouldn't they have the same allowance if they have the same body mass? Why should a large-boned, sensible, middle-aged woman who exercises regularly be told to drink less alcohol for the sake of her health than a desk-bound, shorter, lazy man the same age ?** The more you think about it, the less reason there is to take the RDU argument seriously. It heralded the start of the nanny state, the time when politicians stopped worrying about making sure hospitals were clean and efficient, and started spending millions of pounds on leaflets, websites and public health advertising telling us what to eat, when to exercise, how to stop smoking and how much to drink. Setting a measure like the RDU means the Department of Health can regularly estimate (inaccurately) the number of people who allegedly drink too much and then waste even more of our money on trying (and failing) to

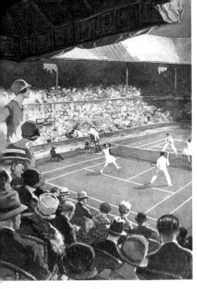

reach them. The anti-drink lobby keeps loads of bureaucrats within the Department of Health in jobs and highly paid men and women heading up quangos. It results in bonkers ideas like the proposal to stop people who drink too much from receiving benefits – and if ever an idea is doomed to fail, it's that one. Of course, there's a small minority of the population who <u>are</u> drinking too much, but if you believe the statistics put out by official bodies, the whole country will be dead within a decade. Are you telling me that as a nation we drink more than in Victorian times, when kids aged thirteen were working as prostitutes, and gin was the drug of choice amongst the working classes? Egged on by government, the media seem obsessed with portraying us as a nation of hopeless drunks **– and it's just not true.**

> The answer to healthy eating and drinking is simple – teach every child how to cook from the age of five, and talk about sensible drinking at school. Education coupled with practical skills changes lifestyles, not statistics and scare tactics.

Anti-alcohol abuse campaigns mirror the government's anti-obesity campaign, which is having virtually no impact whatsoever on the number of fat schoolkids and a whole generation of adults who aren't going to reach for an apple instead of a burger, even if their local health authority promise them cash and vouchers for every pound they drop.

MUMBO JUMBO ABOUT UNITS IS MEANINGLESS

WHAT THE HELL AM I BUYING?

Packaging is one way that retailers seek to completely confuse us with mumbo jumbo. After discovering that shoppers were not buying food labelled 'suitable for vegetarians' because they said it reminded them of tasteless proteins like tofu and soya, there are plans to rename the same products 'meat-free' because it sounds sexier and hopefully will appeal to the fast-growing vegetarian market, which is said to be worth £254 million. The Plain English Campaign says the way many foods are described is 'comical gobbledegook', citing the vast range of ways poultry farmers describe eggs and chickens as completely meaningless. They say (and I heartily agree), 'Food can't just be food anymore. We have to be given the impression it's "more than just food".' Eggs can't just say 'free-range' or 'barn-reared' – increasingly packs are festooned with pictures and potted life stories about the rare breeds and where they live. And when it comes to a free-range or organic chicken, there's more information on some packaging than an immigration official has access to at border control in Dover –

here are a few examples:

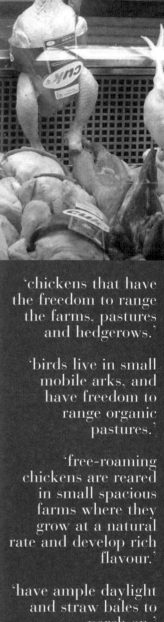

'chickens that have the freedom to range the farms, pastures and hedgerows.'

'birds live in small mobile arks, and have freedom to range organic pastures.'

'free-roaming chickens are reared in small spacious farms where they grow at a natural rate and develop rich flavour.'

'have ample daylight and straw bales to perch on.'

YOU'D BE BLOODY SURPRISED IF A FREE-RANGE CHICKEN DIDN'T ROAM OR SIT ON A BALE WOULDN'T YOU?

CELEBRITIES SPEAK AND WE BELIEVE THEM – WHY?

The charity **Sense About Science** regularly publishes toe-curling examples of celebrities mouthing complete twaddle and claiming it as fact. In a report monitoring the worse offenders, they cited a C4 programme called How Toxic are You? in which the presenter, Sarah Beeny, enthused about 'lovely make-up and moisturisers which don't have any chemicals in them'.

No mention of the fact there are many different kinds of chemicals, both natural and synthetic, and chemicals are present everywhere, even in outer space.

Julia Stephenson, who used to write a column under the irritating moniker The Green Goddess (not very eco-aware when she mentioned she flew to Switzerland for the weekend), once talked about her **'war on electro-smog'** and said 'our unprecedented exposure to electrical equipment, mobile phones and WiFi means we are surrounded by a soup of electromagnetic smog at all times'.

In fact there isn't a single serious study linking normal mobile phone use and WiFi with adverse impact on personal health.

Gwyneth Paltrow spoke at a cancer conference and said, 'I am challenging these evil genes by natural means … I am convinced that by eating biological foods (WHATEVER THEY ARE) it is possible to avoid tumours.' Dieticians say diet cannot prevent cancer.

I could go on and on, but the net result of celebrities making these totally ridiculous pronouncements is that we feel anxious when we shouldn't.

Sophie Dahl told one newspaper she was a vegetarian – then next day another interview appeared in which she said she loved 'cooking a big roast for Sunday lunch'. She seems confused!

IF A FACT COMES FROM THE MOUTH OF A CELEB THERE'S A 50% CHANCE IT MIGHT BE TRUE. OR COMPLETELY UNTRUE.

FEELING STRESSED? GET OVER IT!

A huge amount of mumbo jumbo written over the last few years is advice on how to 'cope' with stress. **Whenever we can't handle something, we describe ourselves as 'stressed'** – but does it really exist as a medical condition?

This modern plague is felling the workforce and costing the economy billions a year in handouts.

Can you believe that over one million people in the UK are suffering from this mystery ailment, which as far as I know didn't exist before the 1960s? Illnesses definitely come and go in and out of fashion. *In the 1990s, one in seven people taking time off work for sickness decided to be suffering from back pain. That figure magically dropped a decade later by more than 40%.* I don't believe that the

design of the average car seat or office chair improved that much, that the workforce have all remembered to bend their knees when lifting heavy objects, or that thousands of middle-aged men and women spend thirty minutes a day performing exercises to strengthen their abdominal muscles. *Forget it.* **We've actually got fatter and flabbier.**

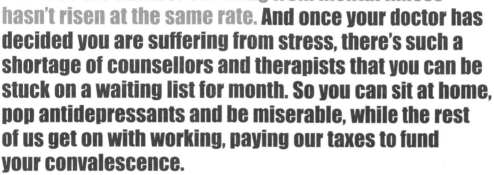

No, there's a new illness to catch, and these days, people who've never even seen a war zone, only the inside of a commuter train or a large office, will generally decide they can't cope and rush off to their GPs to be signed off from work indefinitely, suffering from stress. This is a pretty mysterious because the number suffering from mental illness hasn't risen at the same rate. And once your doctor has decided you are suffering from stress, there's such a shortage of counsellors and therapists that you can be stuck on a waiting list for month. So you can sit at home, pop antidepressants and be miserable, while the rest of us get on with working, paying our taxes to fund your convalescence.

One reason for the increase in people claiming to be suffering from stress is that there is no stigma attached to it. *It's not embarrassing to be suffering from stress, but a measure of achievement, a sign that you've worked so much bloody harder than anyone else in the team.* Stress was once the term employed by engineers and structural mechanics to describe the forces endured by beams with different loadings. Now it's been pinched to describe something vague and all-encompassing, requiring hours of chatting to a kindly psychiatrist. I'm sure that there are deserving cases. I'm sure that it must be exhausting for overworked doctors, faced with a surgery full of miseries, to come up with a way of shuffling them in and out of the door in the twelve minutes or so each patient is allotted. But we must blame doctors for doling out prescriptions

MUMBO JUMBO

for antidepressants, and for signing up to the myth that is stress. Experts agree that the workplace has not got more stressful in the past ten years. If anything, there is now a whole raft of health and safety legislation designed to safeguard the well-being of workers, including legislation relating to noise levels.

A few decades ago our parent's generation stood on assembly lines in draughts and dirt. They didn't suffer from stress. The sad fact of the matter is, most people grow up with unrealistic expectations of what life has in store for them. They don't bother to pay any attention at school, and then are astonished to discover that work is boring and not too wonderfully paid. Most people don't look like those airbrushed pieces of perfection in glossy magazines. Most men haven't got thighs like footballers or the pulling power of a multi-million-pound golfer. Life's like that – unfair. And so, the extremely disgruntled will claim they have 'stress'.

I really resent paying for it, and so should you. Research shows pressure is good for you and can slow the aging process. Taking medication for stress, on the other hand, can kill you.

FROM HEALTH FOOD TO COSMETICS TO PAINKILLERS – WHAT CAN THEY REALLY DO?

Many products that are promoted as aids to dieting have little or no relevant scientific evidence to back up their claims, and when you read the small print it generally says 'works in conjunction with a low-calorie diet and regular exercise' – **we'd all lose weight if we ate less calories and exercised, wouldn't we?** And what about all those products labelled 'reduced fat' and 'light' – they can still be relatively high in fat and calories because food labelling regulations in the UK only apply to stuff labelled 'low-fat' which must contain 3% or less fat. Anything which says 'fat-free' has to contain less than 0.05% fat, although that doesn't mean it contains fewer calories. Indeed, many low-fat foods are high in salt and sugar. **Confusing? It certainly is. You might as well stick to good old full-fat mayo and slap less of it on your sandwich.** And as for yoghurt: stick to plain – anything with a fruit flavour is packed full of sugar. When it comes to painkillers, perception is everything and mumbo jumbo is rife. Research shows we think that taking two big pills will be highly effective – and so most painkillers are sold in packets with instructions telling us to take two at once. In fact, the same dose could easily be incorporated into one small

pill. Many of the more costly painkillers that claim to help revive you include caffeine as one of their ingredients. You might as well drink a cup of coffee. **Face creams regularly make pseudo-scientific claims about how they can arrest the ageing process.**

A beauty article recommending face creams in a magazine described how the new high-tech ingredients in beauty products work:

* Antioxidants: 'round up free radicals'
* Hydroxy acids: 'nibble away at surface debris'
* Humectants: 'draw water to skin'
* Skinbiotics: 'look after your good bacteria'
* Growth factors: 'signal age-weary stem cells to divide and produce new tissue'
* Peptides: 'clever chains of amino acid'
* Hexapeptides: 'tell muscles to stop contracting'
* Oligopeptides: 'repairs netting that keeps skin firm and plump'

Quite honestly this piece could have been written in Kurdish for the amount of sense it makes – it's jargon, pure and simple. The creams that were recommended cost up from £110 downwards. Frankly, you might as well learn to smile more, and keep your saggy chin up in photos – it's a lot cheaper.

LEARN TO LIVE WITH WHAT YOU'VE GOT AND IGNORE MUMBO JUMBO IN ALL ITS FORMS – LIFE'S LESS MISERABLE THAT WAY.

MUMBO JUMBO

SHOPPING

When I was a big cheese in the world of television, we'd waste hours cloistered away in expensive country hotels, soul-searching about what kind of programmes we should be making and how to beat the opposition in the ratings. The most important thing I learned was the art of bullshit – to look good at a corporate away-day or an office morale-boosting session, you have to come up with a buzzword and then get everyone else to repeat it. Once, a bright spark used 'emblematic' as a way of describing our output. Emblematic is simply a posh way of saying 'typical', but it sounds really purposeful and important, and by lunchtime everyone was sprinkling it liberally through their presentations to sound as on-message as possible. Another time, some genius claimed we were too 'remote' from our audience, and that was it, we were using the bloody word for six months, writing it into every proposal as an example of what we were trying to avoid. The same thing has happened in the media when it comes to talking about shopping. Shopping is now inextricably linked to the buzzword of the last 30 years – 'addiction'. Shopping can't be mindless fun any longer, it's got to be studied, dissected, pilloried and, finally, condemned. It's something you've got to give up, get control of, or do in small doses. Nothing too excessive!

Back in the 1960s, any kind of addiction was generally something secret, swept under the carpet. It certainly wasn't part of everyday conversation when I grew up. **Over the last three decades it has become socially acceptable to talk about personal addiction – generally drink or drugs – and how you have overcome it.** Addiction moved to centre stage when famous people not only went to rehab, they actually funded facilities, like the Betty Ford Center in the USA. Some celebrities, like Britney Spears and Lindsay Lohan, seemed to be regularly in and out of various 'facilities' as they battled with all sorts of issues. People such as Michael Douglas owned up to being sex addicts and – the ultimate sign of respectability – several television reality shows have been set in rehab clinics.

Addiction is almost a badge of honour in some circles. **It's no longer enough just to be addicted to crack, vodka, painkillers, shagging or under-age girls;** these days nearly all of us can be included in the latest category of addiction: **rampant consumerism, or shopping.**

Critics say that shopping has stopped being a necessary chore, where you purchase what is needed, and has now become a pastime in its own right. **The word 'need' now stands for the right to buy and has nothing at all to do with want. The anti-consumerists cite shopping as a mind-numbing evil that has stripped the heart out of our city centres and desecrated the landscape with giant retail boxes. Shopping, according to them, is out of control and has replaced sex, sport, conversation and almost everything interesting and rewarding in our lives. Are they right?**

YOU ARE MY ONE AND ONLY LITTLE CAVEMAN!

During the early days of the financial recession in 2008, Church leaders claimed it was morally wrong for governments to tell people to carry on shopping when our level of personal debt is so high. But you could argue that if we stop shopping, thousands of jobs will be lost, the retail industry will implode and many workers in the third world will lose their only source of income. Whole countries in Africa and the Far East now depend on us shopping to keep their economies turning over.

The recession and banking collapse saw the closure of big retailers like Woolworths, changing the character of many high streets for good. In the first quarter of 2009, seven retailers a day were going bust, an increase of 60% on the previous year. **It was said that 50 specialist shops (fishmongers, newsagents and bakeries, for example) were closing in the UK every week and over 40% of our towns and villages now don't have any sort of a shop.** Is this something we should be depressed about, or accept as inevitable?

When you discover that the average person in Britain travels 893 miles a year to buy food, you can suddenly see the potent power of saving precious time and shopping online

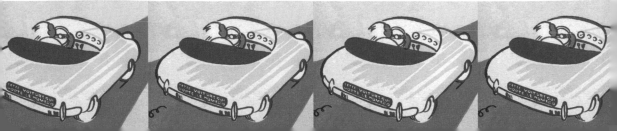

– not getting off your backside, filling up the car with gas or having to negotiate traffic jams and congestion charges.

Even though we may have less to spend, Internet sales are booming (especially on smaller things such as clothes, DVDs, food and shoes, rather than on expensive items like freezers and electrical equipment), and many specialised retailers are easy to find online. **By 2012 it is predicted that 29% of all online sales will be groceries, overtaking electrical goods.** Shopping for food online has become more reliable – suppliers have dealt with complaints about substitutions, food being sent that was near its sell-by date, and damaged goods.

I'm not going to mourn the demise of the high street – it died decades ago, when chain stores took over and the UK became a nation of clone towns, where every shopping centre featured exactly the same handful of dominant retailers, no matter where you were.

Town centres and cities are not theme parks – it is natural for them to alter and change over the centuries. Some people seem determined that shopping should remain in a time warp, where we journey from store to store comparing prices and seeking out bargains. **FORGET IT!** As far as I'm concerned, many high streets have already polarised into charity shops and expensive small retailers – with the middle level of shops long gone. And, although we might think charity shops make high streets look dowdy, they are booming in the recession, with profits over £106million in 2008 – Oxfam alone made £21million. *Back to the anti-shopping brigade – is consuming morally acceptable if you do it in a charity shop?* **I am completely confused.**

Let's take a moment to look at the gradual demonisation of shopping to the point where the once-simple pleasure of spending has been designated the eighth deadly sin. Not so long ago, we were told to junk plastic bags to save the environment, but I can envisage the day soon when anyone carrying shopping will be treated like a smoker – the ultimate social pariah.

Owning up to spending on something that didn't have a reduced sticker on it will be considered as foolhardy as smoking crack.

We seem to have moved very swiftly from a nation of shopkeepers to a nation of people too embarrassed to risk being dubbed rampant consumers by admitting they enjoy the act of purchasing anything. We're being pressurised into giving up impulse buys, fun purchases and spur-of-the-moment whims just as we gave up gas-guzzling cars.

If you don't boast about patronizing a cheap supermarket, or claim to spend hours online trawling for discounts each day, you're simply not on-message in the current climate. I admit, some aspects of consumerism had got out of control: the sight of middle-aged females fighting over tops in Primark and the queues waiting to purchase flimsy Kate Moss gear in Topshop in London and New York was a bit depressing. How many sequined cardigans, denim shorts and fringed suede boots do you need once you've said goodbye to 30? The trouble is, every time we stuff ourselves with pasta or pizza, drink too much and expand a bit around the waist, there is always a cheap clothing outlet to cover those guilty extra inches.

Let's be honest, we have been guilty of buying too much crap.

Shopping for non-essentials had become our drug of choice. But now the pendulum has swung the other way, with a bunch of eco-experts predicting that our shopping is damaging the planet forever. One author, American political theorist Benjamin R. Barber, sees consumerism as a deep-seated moral rot that's corrupting the planet. In his clumsily named book *Consumed: How Markets Corrupt Children, Infantilize Adults and Swallow Citizens Whole,* he claims that an awful lot of products we buy are just not necessary: fast food and many gadgets, for example. He says most people in the developed world already have their basic needs – food, shelter and clothing – catered for, and marketing people are forced to invent new reasons for us to continue to buy. What he calls hyper-consumption has reduced children's lives to shopping expeditions and they identify themselves by brands like Nike, iPod and Coca Cola.

At the same time, adults are encouraged not to be 'youthful', but to remain grownups who behave like teenagers, buying endless new toys they don't need. All of the above is undoubtedly true – parents can testify to the never-ending barrage of advertising and subtle messages pitched at children every hour of the day. The unstoppable rise of television shows such as Top Gear, where fully-grown men clown around like children, shows just how goofy the middle-aged man-child has become.

Attacking shopping is not going to make this all go away. It's not that simple.

Even when you try to buy ethically, locally and frugally, you are still a consumer. Unfortunately for the doom merchants, the signs are that shopping, like alcohol and hard drugs, is a simple pleasure that will never go out of fashion, no matter how many inspiring stories we read about committed souls giving it up for a year and bartering their beans for ironing. At exactly the moment the banks started to unravel, UK sales were only down 0.1% on the previous month. John Lewis, the barometer for middle-class Britain, reported that, although business was difficult, it wasn't catastrophic. Six months later several key high street retailers reported that business had resumed in earnest. The Co-op announced record profits, Next reported better-than-expected results and John Lewis unveiled plans to create 50 new specialist home stores across the UK.

So, HOW TO SHOP and square your conscience with that deep-seated need to own something new or different?

First, it is important to ignore the tidal wave of propaganda that spews from all the major supermarkets as they tout for our custom. They claim to be locked in battle with each other, fighting to offer customers the best value for money. In reality the people they most care about are their shareholders. It is imperative that the supermarkets deliver maximum profits, and that can only be achieved through increased turnover and maximising what you spend. Asda claimed to have reduced 12,500 items in the period up to Easter 2009, but the Grocer 33 price database, which tracks items across twelve categories at all the major retailers, found that only 20% of the items purchased at Asda were cheaper, and half of these items were only reduced in price by 1p.

NOT A LOT TO GET EXCITED ABOUT, IS IT? WOULD YOU REALLY CROSS TOWN TO SAVE ONE PENNY? OR EVEN 10p ON TEN DIFFERENT THINGS? YOU'D PROBABLY SPEND THAT ON FUEL GETTING THERE...

Supermarkets now claim they are dropping BOGOFs (buy one get one free) in favour of what they call 'transparent' pricing – but they seem to be bombarding us with thousands of meaningless small cuts which don't add up to anything important. Meanwhile, food prices have risen 10% in a year because of a weak pound (which has rallied a bit) and high prices around the world for staple commodities like wheat. Our food prices are some of the highest in Europe. And the recession means that even shoplifters have changed their agenda – some supermarkets have started tagging meat, because of a rise in

thefts of basic foodstuffs, rather than luxury items like perfume and DVDs. As people have had less money to spend and can't afford to eat out, sales of own-brand goods and basic cooking ingredients have risen.

For all that I resent their spurious pricing, the ugliness of their buildings and the bollocks they talk about 'saving the planet', I'm not going to give up shopping at supermarkets – it would be like refusing to own a car, a green step too far in this household. And every time I have attacked supermarkets, plenty of you write and remind me you don't have time to shop any other way.

So, how to use supermarkets so <u>you</u> are in control and not them? First of all, you have to plan what you need for a whole week, what you are going to eat every day. If you can cook double quantities for some meals, then you have stuff to freeze and save time later. **The single most important lesson is to have a list – AND TO STICK TO IT. Also, try paying in cash – set yourself a budget – it really focuses the mind.** If you have the time, go online to find details of vouchers and discounts. Always use your loyalty card: you can get money off petrol and you can swap points for all sorts of deals, including entry to family attractions. And beware, supermarkets often post news of bargains and discounts on blogs and chat rooms posing as ordinary shoppers – part of their marketing strategy to direct us towards buying certain products.

Personally, I don't buy fresh food in supermarkets, choosing local shops where it's likely to have travelled shorter distances and I can be sure where my meat, butter, eggs, cheese, vegetables and milk have come from. I shop in supermarkets for wine (often there are good deals), cleaning products, some stationery (but printer inks are always cheaper online), DVDs and toilet rolls. That's about it, but it takes a lot of willpower and planning. You'll save even more if you can go to a discount supermarket and buy this stuff in bulk, provided you've got the storage space. Last time I was in Netto, the pasta was just 19p a bag, so I bought six bags!

Retailers have been quick to seize on the recession as a chance to flood us with feel-good nostalgia – telling us that sales of board games are up 200% (from what level before?).

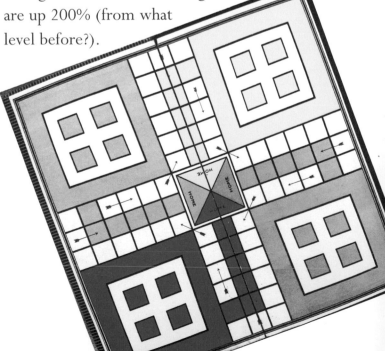

DO YOU KNOW ANY FAMILIES THAT GATHER ROUND THE FIRE TO PLAY LUDO OR SNAKES AND LADDERS OF AN EVENING?

Some retro foods have made a comeback – Cadbury revived its Wispa bar and Bird's Eye brought back the Arctic Roll. Marks & Spencer proudly announced it was selling a jam sandwich for 75p. You could make your own

using less packaging and only costing a quarter of the price. Shops have to find ways of getting us to buy, even if we have less money to spend.

Recent bits of dubious 'news' from the retail sector revealed we are taking fewer baths and more showers (sales of shower gel up). Buying less food at lunchtime and making our own sandwiches (sales of bread, mayonnaise and

spreads up) and (allegedly) cooking more basic hearty fare, like stews (sales of root veg have increased). Sales of custard powders and Bisto are up. In short, the daily propaganda we have been bombarded with about 'superfoods' (expensive berries and green veg like broccoli) has been cleverly replaced by recession-friendly guff about turnips and swedes.

The supermarkets call it 'understanding what customers want'. I call it flogging as much as possible by any legal means.

Fact is, most women in Britain under 30 have no idea what to do with a whole swede or how to cook a turnip, and until Jamie Oliver succeeds in his admirable mission to teach the nation how to eat, and cooking is made mandatory in all schools from the age of eight, ignorance prevails.

So, **armed with your list,** try to time your shopping trip so you arrive when the discount stickers are going on stuff that's near its sell-by date. (I once took a lot of trouble to befriend the bloke in my local supermarket who had the task of slapping reduced labels on the fruit and veg, and he told me exactly what time to turn up each day.) MORRISONS PUTS THEM ON AT 7PM, TESCO AND SAINSBURY'S AT 8PM, ASDA

AT 9PM…of course it might have changed by the time you read this, but it's always worth checking to find out. Don't buy bagged and washed salads, pre-prepared vegetables and washed potatoes.

I always carry a rucksack when I'm walking anywhere in town, so I can buy from street stalls and keep my hands free. But the best way to shop economically is to make a list of the things you ARE NEVER GOING TO BOTHER BUYING AGAIN.

BOTTLED WATER
– what a rip-off.

We drink two billion litres of the stuff in the UK every year. If you drink the eight glasses of water your body needs each day, it will only cost you about £1 for a whole year in your water rates, but in mineral water it could cost well over £500!!! Why do fashionable women want to be seen clutching a bottle of Evian like a life-support machine? Restaurants charge outrageous sums for a bottle of the stuff. Luckily, a successful campaign has been launched encouraging the public to ask for tap water when eating out. Now we need to carry little re-usable bottles of tap water when we walk or exercise. This should be seen as socially unacceptable as carrying a giant designer handbag that cost a small mortgage.

VITAMIN SUPPLEMENTS

There's plenty of research indicating that if you eat a balanced diet, most supplements are a waste of money. The world's largest study, which involved 162,000 women aged between 50 and 79, found that supplements did not lower the risk of common cancers and had no impact on heart disease. We spend a whopping £330 million a year on supplements, money that could be spent on having a good time, clothes and personal treats. The only supplement that has some use is a combination of glucosamine and chondroitin, which helps to protect and repair your joints – 20% of those who took it found some benefit in trials.

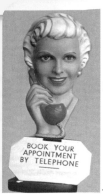

BOOK YOUR APPOINTMENT BY TELEPHONE

OTHER THINGS YOU SHOULD NEVER BUY AGAIN:

SOUPS
These often contain high levels of fat and salt, and even sugar. It's so easy to make your own, there's no excuse. Buy a cheap blender and whoosh soup up at the weekends – using stock cubes is perfectly OK. All you have to do is sweat a chopped onion in oil, add some chopped veg, coat them in the oil, add the stock and then leave to simmer for 15 minutes, and you've done it.

CRUMBLE MIXES, CAKE MIXES, YORKSHIRE PUDDING BATTER MIXES

Why not make your own? – cheaper, and with better ingredients. Simple recipes are easy to find on the Internet. You have to add milk and eggs to most of these mixes anyway.

NEW Wartime RECIPES

Selected by GOOD HOUSEKEEPING INSTITUTE and approved by THE MINISTRY OF FOOD

6ᴰ

SHOPPING, WHETHER MONEY CHANGES HANDS WE ALL LIKE LOOKING AT AND USING DIFFERENT

HABITS A BIT. OK?

GUILT-FREE SHOPPING:

BUYING CLOTHES

The upside of shopping for clothes on the Internet is that it eliminates judgemental or snotty shop assistants. You just type in your size and select. You are anonymous. Anything that looks appalling when it arrives can be easily returned. Just make sure you carefully read the returns policy, and that you get a record of posting when you send things back. In the last year, I have bought a roof rack for the car, books, DVDs, underwear and swimwear, tights, a jacket and some dresses, and ink cartridges for my printer, all online. The hardest thing is to stop yourself clicking that mouse and sending off for something you really don't need and can't afford. And, online, you generally give up your right to haggle. So it might be convenient, but it's not always the cheapest way to buy. Although it involves no transport costs, no parking and no sandwiches or lunches during your shopping trip!

HAGGLING

Clothes shops are quite easy to get discounts in, if you can be brave enough to ask in the first place. Not the big chains like Marks & Spencer, but smaller clothing retailers and shoe stores will often knock off 5–10% if you are buying more than one thing. If something's been on display you might get it cheaper. Haggling is always worth a try, but the trouble is that it just doesn't come naturally to most of us. You could also try for free delivery if you can't get money off your actual purchase.

SPENDING NOUGHT

Finally, try free-cycling. You go online, find the group in your area, subscribe (free) and then see what people want to get rid of. You have to collect it. It's as simple as that. You can post your own unwanted stuff as well. Expert free-cyclers have decorated and furnished their homes this way — spending very little in the process. The beauty of free-cycling is that nothing costs anything, and you are sending less waste to landfill. It's like eBay, but without using cash!

OR NOT, IS A LIFE-ENHANCING PLEASURE.

STUFF. SO LET'S NOT STOP, JUST TIDY UP OUR

grow
your own

food

broken
ankle ↑

Grow your own...

'Celebrity chefs have now made gardening cool again ... growing your own veg is no longer something reserved for the older generation ... not only is it cheap, it can be extremely relaxing and rewarding.'

(Spokesman for Miracle-Gro, quoted in The Daily Telegraph.)

'Gardening? It's just as risky as rugby, say doctors.'

(Report in The Daily Telegraph a few

months later.)

and lose your mind

Rising prices and a recession have seen one in three of us want to grow our own vegetables –

"We'll have lots to eat this winter, won't we Mother?"

Grow your own
Can your own

but do we realise what that process actually entails? TV star Monty Don is a charming man and a wonderful gardener, but he paints a rose-tinted picture of the joys of growing vegetables as if it's some kind of mass therapy, claiming it's a way of 'restoring our self-respect'. During the Second World War Britain's 1.3 million allotments (now shrunk to a pitiful 297,000) formed the basis of

the Dig For Victory campaign – and it's tempting to think that we can dig our way out of the current recession and harness that wartime spirit again.

Trouble is, the previous generation of old-style gardeners were reared on frugality, making and mending, repairing and skimping.

Today we want quick results and no messing about.

YOUR VICTORY GARDEN counts more than ever!

I really wonder if we have the right mindset and enough patience. I grew up in a family where there was no spare cash – and so I saw the trials and tribulations of vegetable growing at first hand. During the Second World War my grandfather turned his back garden in the north London suburb of Southgate into a self-sufficient plot, keeping ducks and chickens and growing enough produce for the whole neighbourhood.

My father made the tiny lawn at the rear of our house on the outskirts of West London into a potato patch, ripping out the herbaceous border and replacing pansies with runner beans. He also had an allotment, which he used as a way of escaping from my mother every evening and most of the weekends when he wasn't being tortured watching Fulham play football. He managed to get a plot at the other end of the park to their ground, and so we hardly saw him as he flitted between these two consuming passions. Now both grandfather and father have departed to that great allotment in the sky, and so my main source of information is the Internet, tips from other gardeners and scraps of paper torn out of gardening sections in the national press.

The government wants gardening to be considered part of the campaign to get the nation fit in the run-up to the next Olympics, but – based on my extensive experience – *it's far more stressful than bloody athletics or cycling.* Having seen the effect this lifelong obsession had on my grandad and father, I resisted growing fruit and vegetables for years, but eventually accepted I am genetically programmed to do so.

Once you succumb to growing vegetables, accept that it's completely addictive – and will entail hours of toil (no matter what Monty and his mates say) and plenty of heartbreak.

My first vegetable patch gave me chronic backache from digging, weeding and pricking out tiny seedlings doubled up on damp ground – I notice all the telly gardening gurus didn't mention that. When I wasn't gardening I spent hours bottling fruit, boiling up chutney and jam, freezing purées, soups and sauces and dealing with the glut my plot disgorged.

MISS RAKE   the gardener's daught

I eventually stopped intensive veg production after eight years in order to regain my health, give my back a chance to rest and to spend some time enjoying life not staring at a row of lettuces. Twenty years later, I have become completely hooked all over again. I'm two years into cultivating another vegetable plot in my garden in North Yorkshire and it's causing plenty of anxiety. **Let's lay a couple of myths to rest: it's no bloody cheaper to grow your own, despite what the experts tell you, and it completely does your head in. You spend months lavishing care on these little sprouting things (plants, not babies) – you urge them to carry on, not give up. You spend money on special feeds you hope will perk them up and make them grow strong. You prop them up with wire, sticks and canes, prune off their leggy bits, spray them to repel bugs, protect them from the elements, and then what happens? Sadly, all that painful work and the hours you've invested will be undermined by two things even the most fanatical control-freak (even yours truly) can't anticipate.** First, *the weather* – it's guaranteed to be crap for a large selection of the crops you've carefully planted and nurtured. If 50% thrive, the rest won't like the wind/rain/heat/frost. A vegetable garden is like a political party – you can't please all the members all the time. Your second enemy will be **pests.** You name them, I've waged war on the evil little buggers – moles, rabbits, pigeons, slugs, butterflies.

A vegetable garden won't just feed your family, it will also feed a massive population of creepy crawlies, birds, slugs and mice. If you think your produce tastes good, so do they.

My sanity completely vanished last summer after a prolonged wet period. *I got up every morning at 7am to kill green caterpillars with my bare hands and drive away the Cabbage White butterflies* who were laying their eggs on my brassicas, cleverly managing to flutter their sneaky way through the triple layer of ugly green netting that might have been a necessity, but which had turned my garden into a plastic jungle. At

the end of a couple of fraught months, what did I have to show for those dawn raids? Just seven cabbages and six cauliflowers. Exactly ten runner beans – I cried as I ripped down yards of perfect leaves from the climbing frame with not a single pod on them. By August I had to go abroad to calm down and spend time horizontal on a sun lounger in a garden with no vegetables (planted by me) growing in it.

I will be embarking on the same roller coaster ride again this year. But don't tell me that growing veg helps me to be a more rounded person. It involves so many emotions, from joy to pride to despair – and large quantities of wine at the end of another session of weeding or watering.

I hope all the new converts who are eagerly planting and sowing for the first time (and promising their nearest and dearest wonderful tasty salads and beans) are mentally prepared for the demoralising let-downs that await. *Just don't cry when you cut your carrots in half and find they're full of weevils, I've been there.* Or when your beetroot stop growing when they've reached the size of a marble. Stop reading success stories in newspapers and magazines, they will just demoralise you further. Don't be impressed by stars like the eco-pensioner Gay Cossins, who spends just £1.42 a day on food, grows all the fruit and veg she needs, makes her own face cream, and brews her coffee out of dandelions (ugh!). Gay looks miraculous for her years, but her kind of

eco-living is a full-time job, involving finding and chopping wood, insulating the attic, tending the garden and foraging for edible plants. **You and I need easy-to-grow vegetables, ones that do allow you to carry on working and earning a living.** Most successful gardeners, you'll soon notice, do it virtually full-time or just hold down a bit of part-time employment. **We need guaranteed results with limited input.**

Growing food shouldn't become another thing you might fail at, like speaking French, driving a car with gears and losing weight.

One way to get better results might be to **garden-share.** In cities over half the homes have gardens, a large proportion of which are woefully underused. Go on the Internet and you'll find plenty of opportunities to **get involved with communal gardening**, where people share the labour and the produce. There have been pilot schemes run by LandFit and Swapaplot, and now the National Trust plans to hand over unused land near their properties which will be turned into allotments (details on their website). There are currently 100,000 people on the waiting list for allotments, so clearly there is a huge demand. As for advice – **gardening blogs can be useful,** because they at least respond to current weather, although you do have to make sure that you understand where the writer is living, because growing seasons vary so much from north to south. Both The Guardian (guardian.co.uk/gardening-blog) and Independent (independent.co.uk/emmatownshend) are useful. I find listening to Gardeners' Question Time on BBC Radio 4 or watching gardening programmes on the television a complete turn-off if you are a beginner – they tend to talk a load of jargon for the already initiated.

Here's how I plan JANET'S WORLD OF VEG – at the start of each year (any time between January and Easter) I make a chart of my garden on one bit of paper. Then I make a list of all the vegetables I'd like to grow on another. Then I look up when you are supposed to plant them out, whether you should grow them from seed and how long their growing period is. Next, I look at the previous year's charts and have a little depressed contemplative time considering my failures (many) and my successes (not enough). Then I take a deep breath, think positive thoughts and on a third piece of paper I construct the JSP master plan, which subsequently turns out to be as f***ing useless as Tony Blair's reasons for invading Iraq.

All this chart-making is more complicated than reworking the Bayeux Tapestry and fraught with unknowns, like periods of flooding, drought, times when I dare to go on holiday and leave the whole lot to fend for itself, losing whole crops as a result.

The seed potatoes I bought cheaply in B&Q were better than the fancy ones I bought from a specialist at twice the price.

Can I give you a top tip? If you see vegetable plants for sale on a stall in a local market, buy them and bung them in. I have had more success with cabbages, cauliflowers and brussels sprouts bought for £1 a bundle in Ripon market than any raised lovingly from seed. Arty-farty designer seed companies are clever at writing up their wares in an enticing way, and you soon discover you've shelled out £25 for a load of packets that contain about twenty seeds in each. Last year I experimented with red orach, a French spinach – very pretty, but only six leaves per stem. *A complete waste of time, you couldn't have fed a bloody dormouse on my output.* Then there was the giant yellow Australian lettuce I was so seduced by on the Internet – a load of floppy, tasteless leaves with no heart.

Won't be bothering with that again.

Gorgeous Italian bean seeds, bought in a trendy deli – couldn't be persuaded to germinate in chilly North Yorkshire, clearly more at home in Napoli.

Top tip – sow carrots in large pots filled with multi-purpose compost. Grown that way, you can eat the thinnings as you go and just leave them in the soil for as long as you like, and the chances of attack from bugs far less. Ditto potatoes: they are perfectly happy in large containers on your terrace or patio, and you don't have them taking up loads of space in the garden. Leeks – again, I buy plants, sod going through the anxiety of waiting for tiny seeds to germinate. Onions – pretty hard to go wrong, as long as you plant them properly and the soil is good. Just don't expect them to get as big as the monsters you see in the local agricultural show. Be happy if yours make tennis ball size, don't be over-optimistic.

You'll gather by now that I am not into anything high-risk. The climate in Yorkshire is mild and wet, so peas, dwarf French beans and lettuces all do well. **I start everything in pots or trays, or yoghurt cartons with holes punched in them.** I accept I look completely demented separating every single seed out with my **£15 luxury Mr Tweezerman tweezers**

(as recommended by all the top models) and placing them lovingly in perfectly neat lines, after which I gently sift soil over them (no nasty lumps and granules the poor little things will have to push against, I want their birth to be as painless as possible).

I worked out the other day that I spend far more care and time on my seeds than on dyeing the roots of my hair ... and it's well worth it, just to see a complete seed tray of perfect

little shoots. Like having a baby, without all the squelching and mess. Don't rush to plant your seeds outside in early spring to cope with unforgiving elements. Last year I boldly shoved my broad beans in the soil in April. **Two weeks later a heavy hailstorm and frost damaged them and they never recovered. I wrapped the shocked little things in straw, begged them to shape up and survive, to no avail.** I had to start all over again and by then it was almost too late – I ended up with just four plants producing beans instead of twenty. *It's so tempting to fill up that dreary patch of soil at Easter, but you have to have self-control in this, if nothing else in your life.* If you are growing vegetables on a balcony, bear in mind that all containers and pots dry out far quicker than anything planted in the garden. The only crop we managed to grow on our terrace in London last summer was tomatoes – although they were plentiful, I found their skins thick and rather repellent.

You can grow lettuces, rocket, mizuna (delicious Japanese peppery salad leaf like rocket) all really easily in shallow containers, but you'll have to ensure that if you ever go away for the weekend, they'll get watered. Or lift them indoors and stand them in a bath.

My top veg has been cavallo nero – a trendy crinkly Italian cabbage, dead easy to grow from seed, frost-resistant and stands in the garden all summer and winter.

I just cut leaves when I need it (same with chard and spinach, both a complete doddle) and I never ever thin lettuces – I always eat the tiny seedlings, gradually making space for larger specimens to develop as the season goes on.

As for courgettes and marrows – how much room do you want to waste? They aren't hard to grow, but they spread. If you can stand the visual nastiness, a growbag is the best bet and doesn't dry out as quickly as a pot.

I'm planning to focus on growing what I think will succeed,

and stuff I can't buy easily – loads of salad leaves, red chicory and small beans and peas. Pink turnips – eating them when they are very small, not like the tired jumbo things you see in shops.

Bitter experience has taught me that what grows well in Tuscany and southern Italy is never going to do anything worthwhile north of Nottingham, unless you have a greenhouse or a disgusting polytunnel. I have invested a bit less than twenty quid in a natty little rack (purchased from Focus using my OAP 10% discount card, which works every day of the week) with a clear plastic zip-up coat over it, in which sit my trays of seeds, my broad beans and peas.

The Royal Horticultural Society gives free advice on when to plant stuff.

1982 GIANT ONIONS never achieved this size since !!

Finally, if you go online, you can find out about seed swaps, where you'll not only meet other gardeners, but can have a jolly good moan about what's gone wrong in your garden. *And don't, whatever else you do, fall for the biggest con of all, buying a jumbo compost bin.* Not only are these large plastic monstrosities repulsive to look at, can anyone tell me how long you have to shove stuff in the top to get anything worthwhile out of the bottom? **I've had more productive relationships in less time than this.** As far as I can see, compost bins are a con, another test of my green credentials dreamt up by the eco-lobby. **Something else I'm no good at. I'm sick of shredding egg boxes, removing anything cooked, taking out anything too fibrous, not putting in too many grass cuttings. The care and time lavished on my recycling bin should be yielding the caviar of composts. Instead, I'm single-handedly supporting a colony of rats and flies.**

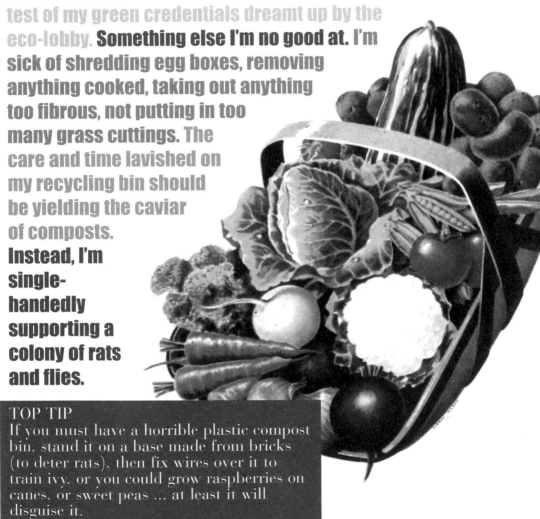

TOP TIP
If you must have a horrible plastic compost bin, stand it on a base made from bricks (to deter rats), then fix wires over it to train ivy, or you could grow raspberries on canes, or sweet peas ... at least it will disguise it.

My mantra: grow your own and be prepared to lose your mind … you'll become obsessed, single-minded and go nuts in the process – but just make a list of all the benefits. On the minus side, yes, it is embarrassing to scream at wood pigeons, kill Cabbage White butterflies with your bare hands, regard slugs as the killer zombies who inhabit your garden … **but here are the bonuses.**

Most important – a carrot doesn't answer back. A lettuce you've grown is sweeter than a kiss. Potatoes you've just dug are better than a date with Mr 40%. I could go on, but you get the picture.

Life's too short not to give it a go

THE NEW YOU

The title is ironic – let's be honest, we know that changing the bits about our lives we're not happy with is very difficult indeed. If it was that f***ing easy to recalibrate our eating/exercising/drinking patterns, how come it's estimated that one in four adults in the UK is overweight and we're constantly being told we drink too much? A big advice industry has grown up over the last couple of decades – telling us what to eat,

WOW!

what to wear, how to get fit and even how to be happy.
We seem to be hopelessly addicted to reading this
drivel, even if the size of our backsides and the rising
divorce rate seem to imply we're not actually turning
words into action. Wouldn't the time we waste reading
this stuff be better spent doing more things that make
us feel good and living a bit more recklessly?
Just a thought!

The recession has meant a double whammy for women's magazines and the feature pages of newspapers. They have had to combine their usual agenda of relentless self-improvement and rabid consumerism with the new mantra of thrifty living. According to many of these self-appointed experts, all you have to do to turn your life around is sign up for any four of the following:

- slap on expensive face cream
- exfoliate those dimpled thighs
- buy an espresso machine
- join sewing classes
- invest in a preserving pan
- eat brightly coloured fruit
- keep chickens
- drink a weird kind of tea
- start a diary of your moods
- use a mini-roller on facial slack
- get on Facebook

And if you do, these experts imply you are guaranteed to cast off your current overweight/ slothful/broke/ spotty/ miserable/non-achieving existence and be transformed into Renaissance Woman: well-balanced, positive, fashionably dressed, gorgeous, and with a bit of cash in the bank. Complete crap, of course, but it hasn't

stopped female writers telling us what we should be doing to be happy
with less cash and the prospect of unemployment.

A pretty typical piece about how to cope with the recession was by Rachel
Cooke in Marie Claire magazine, with the headline

WILL THESE TOUGH TIMES MAKE US HAPPIER?

Underneath there wasn't a picture of Rachel (who's a good interviewer and I don't know why she was writing this bilge), but a photo of a skinny model collecting lumps of wood wearing ludicrous knee-high black socks and a chic outfit, accessorised with a cute dog – implying that to be happy, all you need to do is wander down to the local woods and start picking up sticks. **GET A F***ING LIFE!**
Rachel writes that when she started working from home, she had a big change in her life. **Not earning more/less money. Not worrying about getting a fat arse sitting at the computer all day, churning out fluff like** this. Not loneliness 'cos she wasn't in an office with the daily opportunity to have a girly gossip in the lavs. *No, her big problem was* **SHE WOULD HAVE TO MAKE HER OWN COFFEE.** (Statements like that serve to remind us why more

women aren't running superpowers or developing new technology. The girls are probably in a back room somewhere trying to work out how to operate a grinder and a milk frother.) Rachel solves her big problem by investing in a swanky espresso machine – and discovers she enjoys the whole ritual enormously. Even better, **she concludes that now her morning coffee costs her a tenth of the price it used to when she patronised the likes of Starbucks (exhibiting a shaky grasp of economics) , but more importantly it feels 'quite good'.**

Moral: spend several hundreds of pounds on that special bit of equipment and your life will be enriched.

Warming to her theme of feeling good when things are bad, Rachel reveals that she used to spend over £250 on a handbag, but is now really pleased to see that designers have risen to the challenge of cash-strapped consumers by coming up with stuff that won't date so quickly – **'I look at this season's more discreet accessories – quiet, unshowy, durable – and breathe a sigh of relief'.** Surely this is having your cake and eating it – i.e. saving up for an expensive designer bag, which you justify because it's a TIMELESS CLASSIC. **This is what is known as guilt-free consumption in the warped world of high fashion.** Victoria Beckham – no recession for her – has amassed acollection of 100 'classic' Hermès Kelly bags, *said to be worth a whopping £1 million,* including a silver number studded with diamonds, which set her husband back £80,000 when he bought it for her Christmas present. **Imagine being remembered as a woman who had the most**

expensive collection of handbags in the world – what a tragic accolade. Rachel delivers another pearl of wisdom: **'Who needs a monthly leg wax when every six weeks will – just about – do?'** culminating in the inevitable top tip: **'There's deep satisfaction in make do and mending, finding a bargain and enjoying small pleasures.'**

MAKE-DO AND MEND

Go through your wardrobe

Pass the sick bag.

It's true that recently sales of sewing machines have risen by 45%, and there's been an 84% increase in the number of Internet searches for sewing and dress-making classes – according to one writer **'IT'S SEW CHIC'** to make your own clothes. But is this a by-product of the recession, or more likely, the impact of television programmes like Gok's Fashion Fix, on which Britain's favourite high-street shopper has

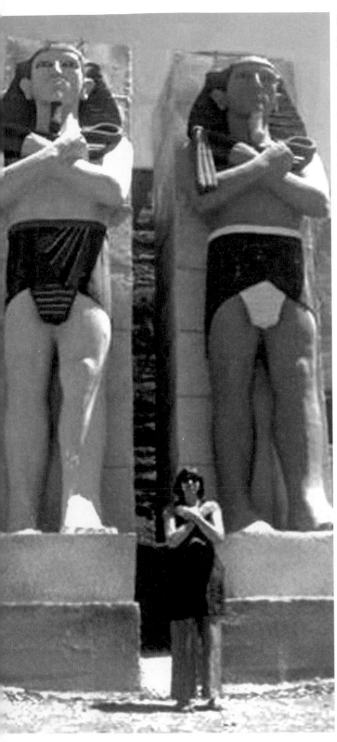

shown millions of women how easy it is to alter and customise clothes to create your own look, without wasting money on overpriced designer clothes? What I really resent is being told by these new high priestesses of thrift that consumerism is evil.

How many women over 30 have the time and patience to work, shop, cook, clean and then find the time to remake a dress? Or to spend hours trawling eBay in search of something gorgeous that's second-hand?

Every time you read that a celebrity is wearing 'vintage' or got her bag or frock on eBay, let me tell you – she didn't. **There will be a highly paid stylist or PA doing it for her.**

The one thing we don't have – apart from money – is time.

And choosing things you can't try on is really difficult – you can waste a fortune buying stuff online that just doesn't suit you. Let's be realistic – sometimes it's better to acknowledge your shortcomings and pay a friend or a dressmaker to help out.

Plus, it's always good to get a second opinion.

Gok Wan is one of the few people who actually practises what he preaches.

The fact is, fashion and beauty editors wake, live and breathe with just one aim: to make us want to buy more stuff.

They have to issue ludicrous dictats about what's in and what's not each season (in spite of the fact that global warming means the traditional seasons have all but vanished).

They live on Planet Fashion, where no one in their right mind would wear something they only bought a year ago. It has to be fresh, new and of the moment, or at least five years old, in which case it magically becomes **'vintage'**.

I turned up at a party wearing a pink lace dress I'd bought in a junk shop for £10, teamed with a pair of black rubber swimming shoes because I'd got a big blister on my heel. A fashion scribe was monitoring arrivals, and I was astonished to see my bizarre combination described as 'vintage' when my picture appeared in a gossip magazine a couple of weeks later.

If you ever get asked where you've bought your frock/bag/shoes, it's always best to reply 'vintage', because that always shuts up your interrogator.

Pretend they cost £10 even if they didn't – there's nothing like a bit of bargain one-upmanship to put you in a really good mood. Fashion editors have a unique way of dealing with the recession – one that you or I will never be able to pull off: they bung on a £1800 ball dress from Dolce &

Gabbana or Chanel (which they got with a massive discount) with a pair of unlaced cheap trainers or a vest from American Apparel. They stick a pair of Marks & Spencer pyjama bottoms with a cashmere sweater from Louis Vuitton. They team a pair of men's boxer shorts with a jewelled corset by Lanvin. *If we tried any of the above, we'd find ourselves in a straightjacket being conveyed to the nearest maximum security mental home pretty sharpish.* These mix 'n' match cheap and luxe combos only work when they are photographed on a camel outside Fez or on a glacier in Iceland. They're not going to get any kudos at the local wine bar or the staff party.

First, fashion editors spend weeks staring at women who look like pipe cleaners marching miserably up and down a catwalk, then they tell us designers have come up with the most unwearable clothes – as in flesh-coloured jumpsuits made of thin silk – and finally, hey presto, six weeks later they are telling us how to accessorise jumpsuits, and calling it **'how to make this season's look work for you'.** They never say anything is shit, dreamt up by a bitter and twisted gay designer on another continent, do they?

THE BEST WAY TO MAKE UNWEARABLE FASHION LIKE CORSETS, PYJAMAS, JUMPSUITS AND SHORTS WORK IS SIMPLE. DON'T BUY THEM AND DON'T EVER TRY THEM ON. LIKE HEROIN, PROFITEROLES AND MEN WITH MOUSTACHES, MY ADVICE IS: LEAVE WELL ALONE.

In the real world, women average a size 16 — but they are invisible in fashion magazines. Love, a glossy new Condé Nast publication, was bold enough to put the outrageous lesbian singer Beth Ditto on their first cover, naked, except for a strategically placed pink tutu. Inside, she wore an elastic string dress by Gareth Pugh and an orange feather skirt by Louis Vuitton — both had to be specially made. Beth is a size 20, proud of her shape, but choosing her as a cover girl didn't mean anything about fashion extending the hand of friendship to real women. **What we wear generally never gets photographed in glossy magazines, does it?** That's why online shopping is booming, there are no judgemental shop assistants. **Since the recession, we've been told that sales of black tights have soared, while brightly coloured clothes, which we might tire of after a few months, have declined. Sales of cheap clothes – from Primark, for example – flattened out in the spring of 2008, but a year later they were starting to rally again.**

For all that's written about sewing, swapping, jumble sales and charity shops, most women over the age of 30 haven't got the time or the patience, and who can blame them?

In spite of what these 'frugalistas' write, most of us like being consumers, even if we have less money to spend.

THE NEW YOU

When it comes to advice about what to eat and how to be fit, we are at the receiving end of even more piffle.

At least most beauty writers aren't going to tell us to make our own creams, though – far from it, they want us to spend more and more. Was it always like this? Look at pictures of your relatives back in the 1950s. **They didn't have magazine or newspaper columnists telling them how to be happy – they just got on with their lives, mucked in, hung out with their friends, lived frugally and put up with their husbands and partners. They ate butter, Spam, loads of white bread, drank Babycham and gin and Dubonnet, and had no idea what a superfood was.**

I'm not saying life was perfect then – but why are we constantly told how to IMPROVE our lives today, as if there is something fundamentally lacking – when there isn't? **Truth is, we have too much of everything now, too much choice in every department.** Bear in mind that most of the 'information' included in newspapers under the guise of scientific fact, is generally from surveys that have been financed by a particular manufacturer or business, with the sole aim of selling more of what they produce. *Every time you read something that starts with the words 'A SURVEY HAS FOUND', you can generally disregard whatever follows as fanciful tosh.*

Every day we are bombarded with spurious information that gradually builds up in our subconscious and subtly undermines our confidence.

FACT: The Guardian newspaper produced a booklet entitled 'How to Feel Good' in association with Müller Vitality, who make yoghurt with sugar in it. This publication contained such pearls of wisdom as: THINK POSITIVELY – BREATHE DEEPLY – DON'T GO TO BED DEPRESSED – DRINK A YOGHURT A DAY AND SEE HOW MUCH BETTER YOU FEEL! USE YOUR EVENINGS – WATCH A DVD WHILE YOU DO THE IRONING – ALWAYS DRESS FOR YOUR BODY SHAPE AND DON'T FOLLOW TRENDS IF THEY DON'T SUIT YOU.

Hardly rocket science, is it?

DRINK TEA AND

CHASE & SANBORN'S "SEAL BRAND" COFFEE

SERVED EXCLUSIVELY AT THE WORLD'S FAIR.

FIGHT OBESITY

(Daily Mail headline). According to Nutrition magazine, white tea (which costs three times as much as normal tea, naturally!) strengthens bones, lowers your blood pressure, prevents the storage of fat and helps break down existing fat that is being stored in the body. This kind of writing implies that the reader is fat and needs help.

Another clever trick is to write about 'changing your mood' – which implies you were depressed or miserable in the first place. According to a nutritionist in The Daily Telegraph, you can 'boost' your mood by eating brightly coloured fruit and vegetables – most contain antioxidants they claim can protect your body from 'free radicals' (WHATEVER THEY ARE BUT THEY SOUND FRIGHTENING) which, we are told, can affect 'your long-term health, and the elasticity of your skin'. The same article recommends eating sardines once a week to reduce the chance of dementia.

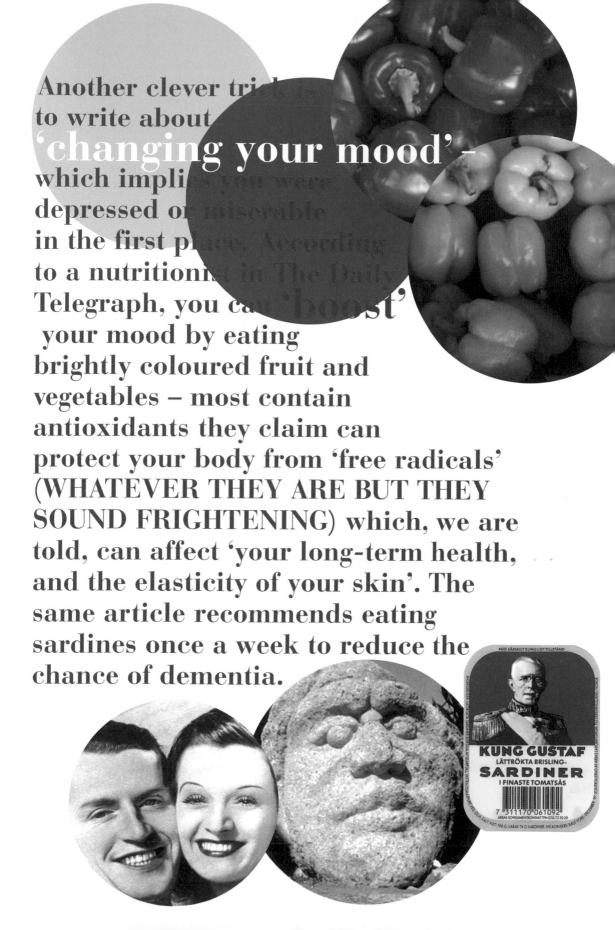

MED SÄRSKILT KUNGLIGT TILLSTÅND

KUNG GUSTAF
LÄTTRÖKTA BRISLING-
SARDINER
I FINASTE TOMATSÅS

7 311170 061092

The London Evening Standard ran a story selecting London's 'top'
therapists and counsellors. They specialised in addiction, anxiety disorders
and positive thinking. One, Dr Linda Papadopoulos, who looks like a
glamorous model and who appears regularly on television, deals with 'body
issues' and was said to charge £145 for 45 minutes. *Most of this
counselling is for conditions – apart from
addiction – which were not recognised as
needing professional (and often expensive)
treatment or counselling a couple of decades
ago.* **Psychoanalyst Susie Orbach has written a book
called Bodies, in which she claims we now see our bodies
as 'projects, not places to live'. There is so much pressure
to conform to unrealistic ideals that many of us think we
are physical failures. She says we are at war with our own
bodies – and she's right. This media preoccupation with
good and bad foods, the right and wrong way to exercise,
the correct and incorrect way to dress, ultimately makes
us unsettled and suspect something is missing from our
lives, when it isn't.**

THE NEW YOU

Then there's the perverse journalism that tells us stuff we were previously told was evil and unhealthy – like butter – has been re-evaluated and is now officially OK. I read one feature claiming that bread, ice-cream, red meat, potatoes and flapjacks were GOOD for us … but don't get too excited, there'll be another article next week telling us the complete reverse. <u>What</u> <u>about</u> <u>all</u> <u>the</u> <u>pressure</u> <u>to</u> <u>exercise</u> <u>and</u> <u>keep</u> <u>fit?</u>

One in eight gym memberships start in January, when you're disgusted with the amount you ate and drank over Christmas and New Year, and every magazine is full of celebrities promoting their exercise DVDs and diet books. By June, however, 20% of us will have stopped going, and by the

following December, only a fifth of the new gym bunnies will still be exercising. It's estimated that we waste £200 million a year on gym subscriptions.

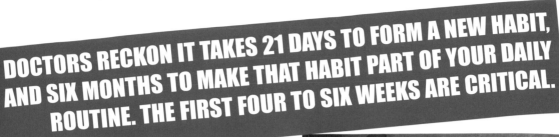

DOCTORS RECKON IT TAKES 21 DAYS TO FORM A NEW HABIT, AND SIX MONTHS TO MAKE THAT HABIT PART OF YOUR DAILY ROUTINE. THE FIRST FOUR TO SIX WEEKS ARE CRITICAL.

Surely, being healthy is a mindset. What's the point of joining a gym if you can exercise with friends, play football, go for a run, do a dance class? Companionship and social interaction is far more important than pounding alone on a treadmill. What's better than walking with a friend, playing netball or rounders, or running after the dog?

WOMEN SPEND TEN YEARS OF THEIR LIVES ON A SERIES OF DIETS

(newspaper headline). Even if this were true, there's no way of really knowing. **It was claimed that between the ages of 18 and 70 the 'average' woman will have tried 104 different diets, lasting around five weeks each, and her average weight loss works out at 6.3lbs. One in four women do all the diets and lose NOTHING AT ALL.** The end result of all this is that now one in four women are actively considering surgery to lose weight.

I've said it before and I'll say it again and again: all this just goes to show that DIETS NEVER WORK.

And why, oh why, spend ten years denying yourself things you enjoy? Eat anything you like, it won't make a blind bit of difference in the long run. And most people who have liposuction put all the weight back on after two years anyway.

The beauty industry

is only obsessed with one thing: getting us to believe that it's possible to turn back the clock. They have correctly worked out that we have a rose-tinted view of our past, and believe we were happier when we were thinner and in our twenties and our skin hadn't started to sag. But then they factor in something else: the idea that everyday life contains so many dangers, in the form of pollution and toxins, that we need cutting-edge technology to protect ourselves. **It's all utter claptrap, of course – good skin is down to genetics, what we eat, fresh air and drinking enough liquid every day.** The only form of protection our skin needs is against the rays of the sun.

Easy Living Magazine asked its readers:

How far would you go to stay young?

They talked about human growth hormone, which stars like Debbie Harry and Sylvester Stallone swear by. I've interviewed Debby Harry and her skin is certainly no better than mine, and who would want to look like Rambo? We are told that CRON (calorie restriction with optimum nutrition) is a regime that its fans claim will lengthen their lives – but it involves eating a third less than the recommended allowance, so way below 1500 calories a day, and existing on a diet of vegetables, fruit and beans.

PUT **GLAMOUR** *in* **GREY** AND GREYING **HAIR**

Smoke COLOUR RINSE

Gives a youthful sheen in any shade of glamorous *natural* grey (no blue or mauve). A "Simple to brush-on" rinse—no staining or dyeing of hair, scalp or clothes.

5'6 per bottle (Several applications)

MEN like Smoke It's so natural-looking. Ask your husband to try it.

A Harlene PRODUCT

IS THAT HOW YOU WANT TO SPEND YOUR SEVENTIES AND EIGHTIES? EATING SEEDS? I CERTAINLY DON'T.

The problem with this kind of journalism is that it is predicated on just one thing:

WE MUST AVOID DYING AT ALL COSTS. Talk about ignoring the inevitable.

The jargon they resort to is totally impenetrable, talking about things we've never heard of, from free radicals to antioxidants. **Nothing can stop your facing sagging short of a face-lift – it's just a sad fact of life, although spending time every day grimacing and performing facial gymnastics may tighten certain muscles. And when you read the list of ingredients on many products (listed in order of size) many start with aqua – which is water.**

Nevertheless, there was a huge fuss recently about Boots' so-called wonder face cream Protect & Perfect Serum. The company submitted the product to a clinical trial and then proudly told the world that 43% of those involved saw a noticeable difference in their wrinkles. But when you read the small print in the research, it turns out that only 60 people took part in the trials over six months, of which half used the real cream and half a placebo. I reckon that 43% of thirty people means that just thirteen saw a result – and that's hardly enough to merit rushing out, slapping on Perfect & Protect for six months and expecting your wrinkles to vanish.

The truth is, a creme such as Boots' No7 Protect & Perfect serum cannot stop your skin sagging, even if for some people it MAY reduce the appearance of wrinkles. (The actual number of people who noticed this result in the tests was tiny – a high percentage of a small group, sure, but certainly not dozens or hundreds or thousands.)

One cheap way to possibly slow down a sagging chin is to treat your facial muscles the way you do your abs or your backside and use exercise – needless to say there are facial trainers available at a whopping £95 a session, or you can buy a book and attempt them in the privacy of your own home, as they make you look like a gurning lunatic. All sorts of gadgets claim to be able to stimulate your facial muscles into perking themselves up; the cheapest is a little roller for £20.

This unending quest for personal perfection made *The Source*, a self-help manual, a best-seller in the US. Written by Woodson Merrell, a specialist in integrative medicine (whatever that may be), the book was avidly taken up by women's magazines everywhere, who enthusiastically repeated Mr Merrell's life-plan under the heading

TURN YOURSELF AROUND IN THREE WEEKS You had to give up red meat, alcohol, coffee, processed food, wheat, cow's milk, sugar, white rice and potatoes. Instead you could eat organic vegetables, fruit, fish, nuts and seeds, get eight hours' sleep a night and take plenty of exercise. This is a completely unrealistic agenda for most people – and yet thousands bought the book, seeking that

holy grail of A NEW YOU. You might turn yourself around, but – exactly like endless dieting – I guarantee that two month later you will have turned around all over again, back to exactly where you were in the first place.

DON'T FALL FOR THE IMPOSSIBLE DREAM OF CREATING A NEW YOU.

LEARN TO LIKE YOURSELF JUST THE WAY YOU ARE.

It's cheaper.
It's less demanding.

It's a lot
more fun.

The New

When Mrs Beeton wrote her best-selling *Book of Household Management* almost 150 years ago, she believed the key to running things efficiently, within a budget, was to set out rules and make sure everyone knew what they were. She also outlined a strict code of etiquette, with instructions for how to behave in every conceivable social situation – it was important that everyone felt comfortable, no matter what they earned. Like the Victorians we need to adapt to the new mantra of frugality – but how?

Etiquette

Schmuck's Mop Wringer.

We've spent so many years living off our credit cards that the idea of saving, not spending, is hard to grasp. **And there's another problem: we've become so very good at putting ourselves first, making sure we've got the requisite amount of 'me time'** (which we deserve as a reward for working so f***ing hard), **that we're totally relaxed about letting the kids get their own food, buying ready meals they can bung in the microwave. We work long hours – so we can't be arsed to waste our free time cooking, cleaning or listening to our partner whingeing on about the boring minutiae of their world.** But once you find out that you've got less money to spend on yourself after paying to heat your home, you'll have to accept that attending yoga classes, buying shoes off the Internet and booking mini-breaks in Tuscany will be a thing of the past.

The day has come when you must face reality: you're broke. But then, so is most of Britain. The days of inviting mates round to slurp your nice wine and dine on a menu you culled from Gordon Ramsay's or Jamie Oliver's latest book are over. You still want to see mates and socialise – but at a tenth of the price. **Buying a new dress for a friend's wedding – forget it.** How do you return hospitality? What to give at Xmas? There are thousands of dilemmas you'll be facing every day. In a moment, I'll offer you some thoughts based on how I (and my friends) manage. You may no longer be able to save loads of cash for your retirement or a swanky holiday, but you will be saving face. There's another plus: look on this enforced austerity as a chance to cut the crap (and the boring people) out of your life without causing offence. But first, you have to alter the focus of how you spend your time. In short:

LOVE WHERE YOU LIVE

One of the things about modern life I find very strange is the small amount of time we spend at home. Think about the huge proportion of our earnings devoted to buying or renting somewhere to live. **After hours slogging away at work earning this cash, what do we do? Go out – it's the ultimate paradox.** We go for drinks on the way home with workmates to moan about how crap our job is. We meet up with our friends every week to moan about how crap our workmates are. We join our partners for cheap meals at the local pizzeria or wine bar to moan about how crap our bosses are and how we're undervalued. We rush off to yoga/pilates/spin classes to wind down after a stressful day at work and then grab an overpriced ready meal to bung in the microwave when we get home. I was as guilty as anyone of all the above — my mantra for most of my life has been **WHY BE IN WHEN YOU CAN BE OUT?** Even when I'd spent years building a brand new house from scratch, designed by an old friend and built by another — a house that the BBC made a film about and the public would write fan letters to — what did I do?

JSP's dream house

Spend nearly every night in a restaurant or down a club, sitting around in a darkened room, hoping to meet Mr 60%. MADNESS! I would get dressed up and rush off to art gallery openings, the theatre, new places to eat, charity events. My diary was packed with things I'd decided to do. It took me several decades to realise that spending two consecutive nights at home isn't a sign of social failure. I was convinced that if I was in, I was missing out on something and somebody, and that my brain would atrophy from lack of input.

Guess what?
I wasn't and it didn't.

I finally got to my fifties and managed the impossible – two nights spent in my own home IN ONE SINGLE WEEK!

I know it's pathetic, but what I suffered from is very common – this fear of social failure, fear of being a sad, lonely singleton, fear of being thought boring. A Johnny no-mates who's anxious that they aren't getting invited to the most happening parties. And if you work from home (which I do a lot of the time), you are so sick of talking to your own fridge and checking your emails hourly that even a trip to buy the morning papers or a carton of yoghurt turns you into a babbling idiot, talking incessantly to anyone who'll listen, just to get a bit of social interaction. These days, I feel like someone who's been through rehab – proud to be able to control my deep-seated and desperate urge to be social. I've got it in check. I still consider going out, but I don't feel I definitely need to.

I have learned to say "No, I'm not available".

The stack of CDs I bought and never listened to during the decades of frenetic socialising are gradually getting played. Ditto the DVDs. The piles of books that built up either side of the bed and on every table are gradually shrinking. For the first time in my entire life, I've sat on my sofa for longer than a news bulletin and I've gone to bed and enjoyed a book instead of some notes I needed for the next day's work.

STAYING IN IS THE NEW GOING OUT.

You know why? The recession has meant we have to refocus things, get our social ambitions scaled down to what we can afford. Our friends are in the same position, so what better time for a reappraisal? To achieve my goal of spending time at home, I had to embrace one difficult new idea.

Remember when we were little, how we sneered at women who described themselves as HOUSEWIVES? Well, take a deep breath, it's time to re-learn the long-forgotten art of being proud to look after and spend time in a home. This is anathema to most women under 70. We have been brainwashed and reared from childhood to think that talking about, let alone owning up to doing housework is demeaning, degrading and not worthy of us. I'm a great example. I loathed the term housewife so much I ended up in a book of

famous quotations with my pithy putdown: 'I hate the term – it sounds as if a woman is married to a house, not a bloke.'

NOT ANY MORE – I put my hands up in shame, we can all make mistakes. After four husbands and I don't know how many men, all I can say is that there's a lot to be said for investing your time, energy, passion and commitment in running a house! It doesn't answer back. It doesn't lose interest in sex. It doesn't get middle-age spread – in fact, the more time you invest in it the better it looks. Your hard work rewards you with a comfortable, non-judgemental cocoon where you can rest and regroup, realise your true personality. In short:

HOME IS WHERE YOUR HEART IS.

I used to stay in because I was too knackered to go out. Mentally I was just staying in to recharge my batteries, not for the positive pleasures of being there.

But that's pathetic – look at all the enjoyable things you could be doing (on a budget) at home. Sex, for example. It's free, if you've got someone available.

The only cost: interesting underwear, decent sheets and the cost of getting them ironed (even we modern housewives don't do that). But there are plenty of other pleasures that don't involve the exchange of bodily fluids or the need to hold your stomach in for half an hour. But first, you have to tweak your surroundings so you find them a cosy and comfortable place to be.

HOW TO MAKE YOUR HOME SOMEWHERE YOU ENJOY
– without spending a fortune

I buy second-hand furniture at jumble sales and little auctions in Yorkshire, and have it recovered in fabulous fabrics. I never throw picture frames away, but re-use them and swap around the pictures in them every few years – old photographs, stuff cut out of old magazines. I buy cheap saucepans and cutlery from catering wholesalers; recycled glasses and water jugs from Tesco; old teapots, jugs and mismatched teacups and saucers, all from house clearance sales and junk shops. Dozens of different dinner plates – none of them match. I've bought old quilts at auctions, and if they're too torn, you can make them into cushion covers. When I travel I buy cheap cotton in street market for curtains and tablecloths – I just cut it and let it fray in the wash, who's going to notice? My bookshelves and kitchen

units are from IKEA, I just changed the handles. I collected 1950s school posters found in flea markets and bric-a-brac street stalls in France and framed them for my bathroom. Old seed packets are framed in the loo.

There's no right or wrong way to decorate – just do exactly what you want and sod the taste police.

And, by the way, forget the notion of starting on serious DIY. There's bound to be a friend or neighbour who can wire a plug or do some painting, or why not offer to swap something in return (a cake or babysitting or gardening)? Life's definitely too short to start buying tools at my age.

Once you're happy to spend more time and less money being at home IT'S TIME TO EMBRACE THE NEW SOCIAL ETIQUETTE FOR FRUGALISTAS.

Here are a few tips:

ENTERTAINING

Let's bring back cheerful meals like shepherd's pie and chilli con carne – cheap, simple to make in large quantities, and easy to eat when you've had a few drinks. Every December I cook my birthday dinner for up to 40 people – it's been Lancashire hotpot, mutton or venison stew (made from cheap offcuts), or chicken and leek pie. All are straightforward, tasty, and hard to muck up. Having a party once or twice a year means you can see a lot of friends in one go and plan it in advance. It could be a summer Sunday lunch or a winter supper. I always make the invites myself and photocopy them. I have my birthday dinner in the local village hall (certainly a value-for-money venue), decorate it with old bunting and fairy lights, lay the tables and do all the serving. For entertainment we have

several rounds of pass the parcel (I make the parcels with old wrapping paper and newspapers, reuse ribbon and string) and musical chairs. **Everyone has to bring a gift (usually an unwanted present) costing less than £10, which goes into the tombola so each guest gets one to take home – the ultimate in recycling!**

If we have a summer supper, we'll play ping pong or have a disco in the living room later – who cares if you look ridiculous – and for dessert we always have trifle (some guests will always be pleased to bring them). I have been known to hold trifle-making competitions. Paul O'Grady makes the best trifle, but he spends about four days doing it! Forget about having loads of different courses when friends come round – make soup and keep it in the freezer if you must have a starter.

<u>Sales of convenience foods have risen 300% over the last ten years – now you have to find ways of cooking that are not just cheaper, but don't take all your time.</u>

I make my own bread on the weekend and freeze it for the week (sales of bread machines have gone up by 50% and it costs much less as well as being dead easy) and always cook using home-made stock from bits of veg and bones. Slow-cooked casseroles and stews are good – make them the day before, they taste better that way. Just make big tins of roasted root vegetables – potatoes, beetroot, parsnips, carrots and onions – cut up into pieces of approximately the same size and briefly tossed in hot oil on the top of the stove before being sprinkled with salt, pepper and a bit of sugar and bunged in a very hot oven for 45 minutes.

Don't be too proud to serve frozen peas – they're delicious tarted up with fresh mint and tossed in butter with shredded lettuce.

I never cook from celebrity cookbooks any more, they involve buying too many special ingredients. I might buy a joint of meat, cut it into pieces, then cook and freeze different dishes. I try to eat vegetarian two days a week. My new favourite is spelt or pearl barley risotto, which only takes 30 minutes to cook. Follow the instructions for preparing the grain, then gently fry chopped onion and some veg, such as beetroot or dried or fresh mushrooms. Add the grain, then gradually stir in the stock until fully absorbed. Chuck in some sage or thyme from the garden for flavour. Serve with a green salad, followed by fresh fruit and cheese – simple!

Two other ways to have fun at home:
card evenings and fancy dress dinners.

I grew up playing cards, and it brings out the horribly competitive side of my character. A small group of us play Canasta every month or so – I roast some chickens (or do one and stuff it so it goes further), roughly cut them up, and put out a buffet with baked potatoes and salad so everyone can serve themselves … and they bring the drink! I don't even bother making salad dressing any more, as everyone's got their own special favourite version. I put out a couple of different oils and vinegars and a lemon, and they can splash on whatever they like – so much less effort than trying to concoct the perfect vinaigrette in a jar.

Once a year I have a holiday with friends, which always ends with a fancy dress dinner – you have to go to the local supermarket and not spend more than twenty euros on your outfit. I usually go as a cleaning lady (I wonder why…?). I adore fancy dress parties – over the years I've turned up as Wonder Woman, Andy Warhol's muse Edie Sedgwick, a runner bean (my friend went as Jack) and Carmen Miranda. Theme evenings are great too, when you re-live the holiday, go through all the embarrassing photos, play those crap CDs you bought in the local market, wear one of your most ridiculous summer outfits, and eat a regional dish.

BUYING PRESENTS AND CARDS

– make your own. Expensive cards now seem vulgar and impersonal. It's good to make Christmas cards, pasting images together and getting them copied, or printing off a funny picture and sticking them on blank cards (such as those from Paperchase). It's not only cheaper but a lot more personal. You can even cut up old cards to make gift tags and save boxes for presents. **Pots of preserves, packed in an old cardboard box you've recovered with wrapping paper, make perfect presents.** I take a rucksack when I'm walking or cycling in the autumn and plan special routes passing fruit trees no one seems to want to pick.

Jelly recipe: Savour apple jelly is fab with roasted and cold meats. Roughly chop up crab or cooking apples, cores and all, and simmer in some water until soft. Strain through a jelly bag (Lakeland sells one) and return the juice to the pan. Add sugar (usually half to three-quarters of the amount of liquid) and boil until the mixture reaches setting point – the surface will wrinkle when you put a drop on a saucer). Stir in finely chopped chillies, sage leaves or thyme and pour into airtight jars. If you're fussy about hygiene (and want to reduce the risk of botulism), and want your jelly to last longer, sterilise the jars first by either boiling them in water or heating them up in the oven.

Then I do some serious foraging – blackberries, damsons, apples, plums and elderberries all make jam and chutneys. **Home-made cakes (the foolproof kind like chocolate sponge or fruit loaf) are always appreciated.**

Sloe Gin is dead easy to make, and you can use bargain gin as the base – it looks so pretty, poured out over ice cubes. Or give a book you've really enjoyed – the chances are your friends will want to read it as well.

RETURNING HOSPITALITY

If you're entertaining, encourage your guests to turn up with something to drink, but stress you want Cava, not Champagne (that just screams 'money to burn'). If you're going out, take your host a plant from your garden (something that splits easily like Hostas, or Dahlias), a bunch of flowers you picked, or a small potted vegetable plant you grew from seed – chilli or tomato or a small pot of baby mizuna. Afterwards, send handwritten notes or postcards, never an email or a text. Be personal, not efficient.

JUMBLE SALES & SWISHING

You can organise your own jumble sale; get a group of friends together and rent a village or church hall – you can always make a donation to a good cause. Announce it in the local paper, stick up a few home-made posters and email everyone you know. This is a great way of getting rid of stuff you can't get over your expanding backside. Swishing is just a modern way of saying swapping – do it online (www.swishing.co.uk), find out where events are happening in your area, or arrange your own.

HOUSE GUESTS

It may sound ruthless, but I have eliminated anything that could be construed as a guest room from my house in London. As I work from home, I don't want to wake up and have breakfast with a friend – it will

only slow my day down and mean I have to be interested in their plans. I don't even have a sofa that looks like you can sleep on it. Instead I negotiated a cheap rate at a local hotel where friends can stay (and if I've invited them down, I'll pay for one night). When I go away I often let friends housesit – it's good for security, and they get a cheap holiday in London and can cut costs by doing their own cooking. Outside London, it's different. I've learned that staying with friends is best kept short, with them wanting more, rather than less, of your company. One or two nights is fine, three is pushing your luck. Take a gift they'll be able to use while you're staying, such as a box of fresh dates or apricots, a leg of lamb, a free-range chicken, or something edible you made. Certainly not bath oil – remember, it's your friend who's going to have to clean this muck off when it's left a greasy ring around their bath.

HAVE TO GO TO A WEDDING/ PARTY/SWANKY DO AND YOU CAN'T AFFORD A DRESS?

1 Don't be too scared to ask your friends if you can borrow something – I am always pleased to lend out stuff to girlfriends who aren't as chunky as me and can get into my party frocks of yesteryear. Just ask them to clean the dress afterwards.

2 Scour charity shops and eBay for something second-hand – the only downside is getting something that won't fit you, and the time it takes trawling through stuff. Top tip: always buy a size too big; most clothes are dead easy to get taken in (and it's not that expensive) but you can't do anything about a dress that's too small.

3 Take a frock in a nice fabric you already have and get a dressmaker to customise it – no one will ever notice and you will be happy for a third of the price. Gok Wan does this every week on his C4 show, using bits and pieces like lace, buttons and ribbons from haberdashery departments (you could buy his books for more ideas). Dressmakers can also lengthen/shorten sleeves, put in contrasting panels, turn baggy trousers into skirts. (You can find a dressmaker via a good dry-cleaners or your local newspaper.)

4 If you already have a dress you like, get it copied in another fabric. There are some great bargains in sari shops – you can buy really cheap material and get it lined if it's going to crease or be too see-through.

5 If you need a wedding dress, there are websites which sell second-hand ones online – why waste money on a new one?

WHAT IF YOU GET INVITED SOMEWHERE BY A MATE AND YOU CAN'T AFFORD TO GO?

Be honest, it's always the best policy. You'd be surprised how sympathetic most people are – if they are your true friends, they will try and find you somewhere to stay in someone's house, see if they can get you a lift with someone else, and they certainly won't expect a present. Just don't ever lie about why you're not going to something – you'll get found out, or your hosts will be offended that you didn't give a good enough reason for not attending.

IT'S PERFECTLY OK TO ADMIT YOU'RE BROKE.

DUMPING YOUR PARTNER

In a recession, it's best to cut out the crap. You could make up a lot of flimsy work-related excuses about how you've got no time for this relationship etc etc. **Your partner is never going to change, and neither will you.** Isn't it best just to be brutal and say you'd be happier by yourself?

'COS YOU WILL BE!

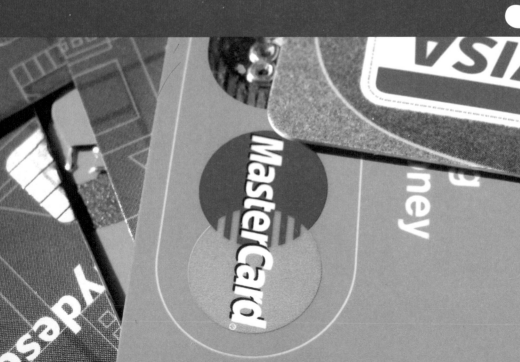

Money

When the shit hit the fan and the financial sector seemed to be in meltdown, I rang my bank for an update. This turned out to be one of those blinding-light moments when you realise that the people you were brainwashed into trusting – those slightly superior beings who gave you such a line about being 'experts' – were actually running around like headless chickens. My 'personal manager' was not in the office, but 'working from home' – so, in desperation, I demanded to be put through to HER boss. I asked the rather emollient chap who took the call if the bank had more in deposits than it did in loans (in other words was it solvent), and after about five minutes of waffle I didn't feel I was getting a concrete answer. I certainly wasn't hearing any reassurances that made me feel better about my pitiful savings.

Thousands of you had similar experiences, and must have come to the same conclusion as me: *how come banks, who we thought were the professionals at managing money, so overextended themselves that we would have sleepless nights about whether they might go bust and take everything we had with them?* We worry about whether we can afford a new car – they seem to have no problem about amassing debts the size of a Third World economy. None of us will ever feel we can trust banks and building societies again – we've seen them shed staff, merge, dump their identities, sack their directors and beg for government bailouts (which means giving them more of our money). They've stopped providing a service and have become a major irritant.

Trust is a word we've had to reconsider in recent times, isn't it? If we no longer trust banks, and rightly think their top executives are overpaid gamblers who take unnecessary risks, what about our elected leaders?

One minute they were telling us to save and were promoting prudence, the next they wanted us to spend our way out of a recession they claimed was not of their making. **If politicians were so good at managing the economy, how come they never predicted the collapse of banks, building societies and the housing market? These are the same mob who (we now know) were living well at our expense, with their noses deeply in the trough, producing receipts to claim that things like jellied eels, Aga servicing, potted orchids, preserving thermometers and treating dry rot were all necessary tools of their trade.** The furore over politicians and their dodgy

expenses claims, and the way many of them were exposed as shameless property speculators, who 'flipped' the residence designated as their main home over and over again in order to minimise paying Capital Gains Tax, has shocked tax payers (who generally don't have expense accounts) to the core. Meanwhile, it's business as usual for many traders and investment bankers – the bonus culture seems to have resumed much as before, while lower down the food chain unemployment is rising.

What bankers and politicians are really good at is blaming someone else.

There are two parallel worlds: one inhabited by the people who seem to get away with murder, and the one in which the rest of us agonise over our tax returns and worry about our pensions. After saving money for 40 years towards a pension, I received a letter the other week telling me that the £180,000 I had saved was now worth £131,000. Not that I actually believe the piece of paper anyway. In spite of claims that they have rewritten pension and mortgage advice forms in plain English to make them easily understandable, I don't know anyone who can decode what their pension projections actually mean. (ANSWER: GENERALLY ABOUT 20-30% LESS THAN YOU THOUGHT).

I'm not stupid, I've run several large businesses, but when I meet my financial advisor once a year and she starts talking about pensions, I glaze over. She might as well be talking in Urdu. I'm one of the many mugs who did what we were told, and saved for my retirement – the trouble is that many pensions have delivered such a poor rate of investment you'd have been better off putting your money in property.

And we live in a two-tier society: the number of public sector workers in the UK has grown exponentially over the last few years – the lucky sods have protected pensions, security of employment and regular pay increases linked to inflation. In the private sector, people are being asked to work the same hours for less money and take unpaid leave. You haven't noticed any bankers or MPs doing that, have you? Or many council leaders, BBC senior staff or NHS chief executives, come to that.

CUSTOMERS – WE'RE THE NUISANCES THAT BUSINESSES WOULD RATHER DO WITHOUT

Those two key words, customer and service, no longer sit side by side in the 21st Century. **We're the customers – but the people we deal with have no concept of what providing service means. How would some untrained school-leaver working in a shop, building society, hotel reception desk or department store, have any notion that we should be valued, cosseted or treated with respect? Banks are another case in point: many of their customer services are outsourced to the Third World – and that's a recipe for disaster. No one has any authority to make a decision, as they seem to operate according to a rulebook dictated from afar.**

In addition, there is zero flexibility about small overdrafts, and their charges are outrageous, prompting a series of legal challenges mounted by campaigning consumer groups. (Google 'my bank charges are unfair' to find out more.) And if you try to call your bank to make an appointment, you get a person you've never met who has to ask a supervisor.

If you want to borrow money, they're likely to take the deeds to your house as security and treat you with utter suspicion. Try Internet banking and you soon start getting junk emails and begging letters from Africa. Credit card companies are even worse: if you complain you're routed to a call centre where they sound like zombies reading from a pre-prepared script. These poor people are trying to mop up the inadequacies of a poorly regulated, badly run financial sector, and they probably earn less per month than a cleaner in the UK.

Rail enquiries are routinely dealt with by people sitting in a room thousands of miles away on another continent – they wouldn't know Kings Cross from a box of matches. They've never been to Swindon, Paddington or Basingstoke. You probably know more about the bloody reality of the rail service in Britain than they ever will, living as they are in Mumbai, Calcutta or Bangalore. Black cabs in central London are booked by workers in a call centre in a remote part of Scotland – they probably wouldn't know Balham from Barnes.

Another guaranteed irritant is **insurance** – how many unsolicited letters do you get flogging insurance on everything from drains to flooding to central heating systems to cars to house contents? I guarantee that when your boiler explodes and you manage to navigate your way through the snotty women on the other end of the 0800 number, they will triumphantly tell you it's not covered by the small print. Or that you have to have it serviced every year (costing hundreds of pounds) before the policy is valid. And if your boiler is over five years old, when the engineer eventually arrives, they just laugh. They try and con you into buying a new boiler, as the old idea of repairing a gadget is rapidly becoming obsolete. Whether it's unjustified parking tickets,

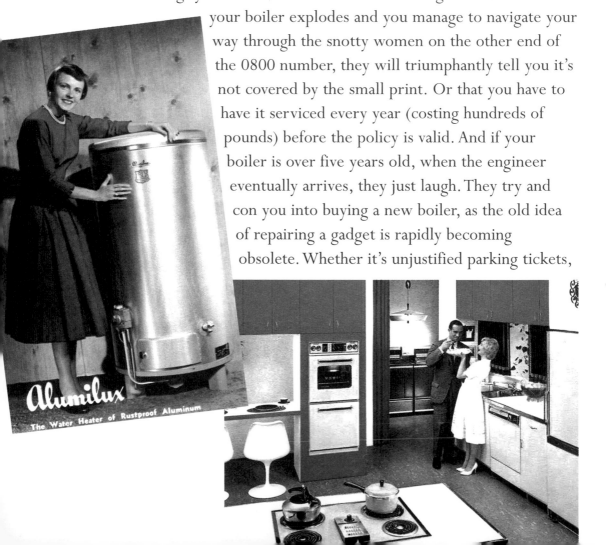

Alumilux
The Water Heater of Rustproof Aluminum

unpaid bills or financial penalties caused by cheques getting lost in the post, the customer is routinely assumed to be guilty until hours and hours have been spent proving their innocence.

My advice is to drastically simplify life. Have as few credit cards as possible. Have as little interaction with your bank as you can manage. Use the Internet to compare insurance rates. Find out what consumer groups offer unbiased advice. Cut out unnecessary standing orders. Over the last decade we have been encouraged to borrow cheaply and buy whatever we wanted – having run up the highest levels of personal debt in Europe, now we've got to manage our borrowings so that we still have a reasonable lifestyle. It's not easy.

MAKE A SIMPLE PLAN THAT SUITS YOU

According to money-saving experts like Martin Lewis, there are two ways to run your finance: *Old and New style.* **Old style** disciples model themselves on their grandparents' generation, where thrift and living within your means were considered the best way to get through life. They collect vouchers and coupons, set targets they will save for by putting away small amounts each week, and think nothing of cooking from scratch, using cheap, own-brand products. They have been scaling down their purchases generally to consume far less. **New style** believers don't want to alter their lifestyle this radically, so they do things like switch mortgages, swap energy suppliers, change credit cards and generally flip their debts around to manage them better. **But they don't give up holidays, shopping and nice clothes; they just spend longer working out how to get things for less and manage their existing debts.**

There are plenty of websites now to guide you through this (listed at the end of this book) but in truth, I think most of us adopt a more mix-and-match approach. It's hard to scale down being a consumer: I'm just

not prepared to stop shopping, but at the same time I don't want to waste my money on things I might be able to get cheaper. I want it both ways – and so, I suspect, do most of you. It's all very well for these money-saving experts to get a thrill out of chiselling 5p off something, or to endlessly rotate their banks, credit cards and energy suppliers, but in the end, you have to ask yourself

HOW MUCH SPARE TIME DO YOU HAVE FOR ALL THIS?

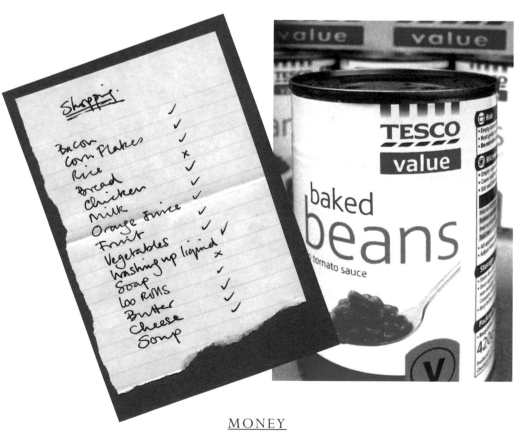

Quite a lot of old-stylers might be retired, and they're more able to find the time and the necessary patience to spend hours online comparing prices, collecting discount vouchers, tracking special offers and shopping around. Money-saving experts do it for a living, and they have to amaze us by coming up with new wheezes and deals all the time to keep their profiles up and their websites exciting and a must-read. For most of us, though, the huge amount of form-filling required when you change your insurance, mortgage or bank reminds us of all the things in life we hate – school, exams, moaning parents and job applications. *Nothing makes me feel queasier than a great big form which starts with the single demand that raises my temperature to boiling point:* **DATE OF BIRTH ...** followed by **MS/MRS? SINGLE OR DIVORCED?** **Why is it so important to know whether a woman is single or divorced? What if you are single, divorced and living with someone? And who gives a f*** whether you are addressed as Miss, Mrs or Ms? Personally, I'd rather be called MADAM over everything else.** All this guff seems to be a hangover from the days when men were breadwinners and women did the washing-up. Any money-saving which starts with a big form won't be top of my priorities. So what's the best strategy to adopt?

The recession has meant that the pages in newspapers that once were called 'personal finance' and were about mortgages, pensions, and savings, are now packed with tips about making extra money or reducing your outgoings. Sadly, it's perfectly obvious that quite a few of the journalists writing this crap have no idea of the real world.

Here are some of the more ludicrous suggestions I've collected over the last few months:

- **EARN EXTRA MONEY BY BECOMING A DOG WALKER ... YOU CAN GET UP TO £10 AN HOUR PER DOG.**
- **RENT YOUR HOME OUT FOR PHOTOSHOOTS.**
- **BECOME A TUTOR – EARN UP TO £25 AN HOUR COACHING KIDS THROUGH EXAMS.**
- **GO TO MCDONALD'S TO SEND EMAILS BECAUSE THEY HAVE FREE WIRELESS.**
- **BUY CHEAP SHOES BUT PUT EXPENSIVE INSOLES IN THEM.**
- **GO INTO SHOPS IN THE MIDDLE OF THE WEEK WHEN THEY ARE EMPTY AND HAGGLE.**
- **DON'T DEVIATE FROM YOUR SHOPPING LIST**
- **COOK USING THE INGREDIENTS YOU HAVE IN THE FRIDGE/STORE CUPBOARD.**

No dog too big
No dog too small

DOG WALKER

Stop me and ask for rates

What you really need to do before anything else, is change how you think.

YOU MUST NOT BUY THINGS TO MAKE YOURSELF HAPPY – IT NEVER WORKED BEFORE AND IT WON'T WORK NOW. ESPECIALLY IF YOU LOSE YOUR JOB AS YOU'LL HAVE EVEN MORE DEBT.

IF YOU'RE MISERABLE, DON'T SHOP, TALK TO A FRIEND. IT'S CHEAPER AND WE'RE ALL IN THE SAME BOAT.

Job security is a thing of the past. Instead of moping, you've got to accept the notion of scaling down what you're going to spend, so that you may even be able to hoard a small amount of savings in case it all goes pear-shaped and you're unemployed. This process can be enjoyable in a smug kind of way – that's perfectly acceptable. It's not a prison sentence. There is pleasure to be had in making your earnings work harder. But you have to be realistic about how much time and effort you can allocate to economising before you get resentful and it becomes counter-productive.

> RUN YOUR MONEY LIKE YOU RUN YOUR RELATIONSHIPS – TAKE CHARGE AND DON'T GET PUSHED AROUND BY OTHER PEOPLE

LIFE IS TOO F***ING SHORT to sweat over saving 10p, isn't it?

MAKE A BASIC BUDGET

You do have to spend a bit of time working out how much money you earn and what your outgoings are – which isn't as simple as reading bank statements. You need to collect all your receipts for a month (or three if you pay some bills quarterly), look at what you spend and divide it into categories: the basics, like rent or mortgage costs, fuel, water rates, council tax. What you spend each week on buying food. Transport costs. Then there's communications (phone and Internet) and satellite television charges.

Finally, make a list of the luxuries like new shoes, CDs, perfume and trashy magazines you have bought. Eventually, you'll have a better idea of whether you can make savings in some areas, how much you can allocate each month to non-essentials like cosmetics, clothes, books and DVDs. Plan to save a small amount for long-term aspirations like holidays and presents. Put your earnings in one bank account, open a second to pay all standing orders and household running costs, and a third account into which you pay yourself a small salary each week. That's your spending money. All this sounds far more complicated than it is. I pay myself a wage, as it's the only way to stop splurging the VAT money on a dress. Stop being fined for late payments by setting up standing orders to your credit cards, no matter how small the amount. Get a new credit card that will pay off the debts on your old card for you – check with money-saving websites to get the advice about how to do this, or go to the Citizens Advice Bureau.

BE IN CONTROL WHEN YOU SHOP

Eliminate that quick-fix act of desperation when you buy something in a panic, and consequently run up a debt you could avoid. **When it comes to buying food, you can shop in two ways: buy long-lasting basics in bulk; buy perishable goods weekly with cash. You can get wine from a discount supermarket which you visit once every two months. Only fill the car up with petrol when you pass somewhere cheap. Shun overpriced designer cosmetics – buy hair and make-up products from supermarkets or online. Buy your shampoo and hair products from professional suppliers like Sally – you can pick up excellent shampoo in huge containers that will last a year.**

EATING OUT

If you eat out, you can save by drinking house wine and never ordering bottled water. Meet friends straight from work and eat early in the evening (before 7pm) when most places have a cheap offer. And if you want to splash out, drink Cava or Prosecco – most people can't tell the difference between a £5.99 sparking wine and Champagne anyway, no matter what you read to the contrary. Cheers!

SAVE ON ENERGY BILLS

I know it sounds pathetic, but how many women can understand their central heating controls? Like mammograms, these are unpleasant pieces of gadgetry designed by men, invented to confuse and annoy most women and quite a few men (although they will never admit it). They rank as one of the most user-hostile pieces of household equipment. Have you noticed how you have to set each bloody time for each day and then copy it for every single day of the week. Don't even get me started on things like 'slumber' or 'holiday settings'. I have run £40 million budgets in the media but I can't run my central heating economically. It's either on or it's off. Set the wall thermostat really low in summer and hopefully the bloody thing won't come on anyway. Or pay some cute technical person to come round and set it, leaving a card with all the settings glued to the front of the boiler.

Check the websites of organisations such as WarmFront and the Energy Saving Trust (see *Useful Addresses, Further Reading, Advice etc.*) to find out if you are eligible for grants to insulate your home. They also provide invaluable advice about how to cut your energy bills. All light bulbs, wherever possible, have to be low-energy, even if it means spending more in the first place. And when you go on holiday, buy those cunning little timer plugs so that a couple of lights go on and off each day.

CUT UP THOSE CREDIT CARDS

I've cut up my store credit cards – that way I can't be tempted to use them when there's a sale or special offers. You can use pre-payment cards (Visa or Mastercard) if you really are determined not to exceed your budget. Set your credit limit really low and if you get asked if you'd like to increase it, just say no. Only use one credit card – that way you incur lower charges – or just use debit cards.

GET RID OF ALL THE CRAP YOU'VE GOT

For years, I rented two storage units, and they were full of furniture I didn't use, books I didn't read, old letters I'd forgotten about, and gadgets I've never worked out how to use. Storing this rubbish cost me about £100 a month! I looked in the local papers and directories for antique and second-hand furniture dealers, and I dragged some of the best stuff out of the units, photographed it and emailed the images to the shops, adding what prices I would settle for. They came and had a look and picked some bits out – I got rid of a sofa, a set of 1970s shelves, a couple of lights, some mirrors, and made about £500. I got a friend to sell my old clothes on eBay, and take a commission (half) – but there are plenty of sites that can do that for you these days. I set up a stall in the village hall the next time they had a fundraiser and flogged my crap as 'celebrity jumble'. Don't knock it – we raised about £300 for their new roof. If you are feeling less charitable you can do car boot sales or street markets – my sister and I used to love having a pitch, regularly raising over £200 each time. I've sold old luggage, trainers, high heels, hats and winter coats. **There's nothing sexier than having a big bag full of coins at the end of a jumble sale or car boot sale!**

MAKE A NEW MOTTO:
IF I SELL TWO BITS OF DETRITUS THEN I CAN TREAT MYSELF TO ONE!

That way you can still browse flea markets, junk stalls and auctions, but the overall total of stuff you've got will slowly decline.

Consuming is so very addictive, and it takes years to wean yourself off it. We've been brainwashed to believe that we need 'new' outfits, 'new' bags and 'new' shoes to impress people. Believe me, they never notice. A new lipstick would have just the same effect.

SMALL STEPS THAT ADD UP

* Cancel gym membership – buy some free weights and rubber resistance bands from Tesco, keep them by the bed or where you sit at the computer, and do thirty reps a day. Get off the bus or train a couple of stops earlier, and that's your workout!

* Don't buy expensive cleaning products – it's been proved (by Which? magazine) that washing-up liquid cleans carpets just as well as most products sold specifically for the purpose. You can use it for most cleaning jobs, washing the car and hand-washing most of your delicates.

* Turn off your mobile for a day at the weekend.

* Have your hair cut after work in the middle of the week by trainees – generally they're more up with fashion anyway.

MY NAME IS JANET, I USED TO BE ADDICTED TO SPENDING MONEY – BUT I'M IN RECOVERY.

Do one SMALL thing every day to save money!
    You'll sleep like a baby x

Greenwash

'Only
one in ten consumers
actually trust green information
from businesses or the government, and
half of us have no idea what to believe about
issues like climate change. Retailers have
latched on to the fact we want to be green – nearly
£17 million was spent on ads using the words 'CO$_2$',
'carbon', 'environmental', 'emissions' or 'recycle' in
the year up to August 2007. The figure in 2003
was just £448,000. Greenwash may cause
consumers to mistrust every
green claim, no matter
how justified.'

(From a report by communications
agency Futerra)

For a year now, I have been chucking my kitchen waste into a large, ugly, plastic compost bin in the garden. Occasionally, when I remember, I get the packet of Garotta (a product meant to speed up the process) and sprinkle some on the stinking pile of potato peelings, cabbage leaves and carefully shredded egg boxes. I must have dumped a ton of garbage in this bin over the past twelve months, *AND YET IT STILL ONLY COMES UP THE INSIDE TO EXACTLY THE SAME BLOODY SPOT.* IF ONLY ALL THE FOOD I HAVE EATEN OVER THE LAST TWELVE MONTHS WOULD MIRACULOUSLY SHRINK DOWN IN THE SAME WAY AS IT PASSES THRU MY BODY INSTEAD OF TURNING INTO A DISGUSTING ROLL OF FLAB LIVING WHERE MY WAIST ONCE WAS.... MAYBE I SHOULD START EATING GAROTTA AND QUIT COMPOSTING.

The idea of recycling, not wasting stuff and producing free compost to use in the garden and for growing organic vegetables is very appealing, if you want to flaunt your green credentials. After all, **green is the new black,** and everyone boasts about having a compost bin, a solar panel and plenty of energy-saving devices. **Composting seemed an easily achievable green goal. At least, it was until last week when I opened the lid of the ugly bin and nearly got suffocated by a cloud of small flies that swarmed out and sought refuge in my hair. At the same time a large rat ran over my foot – it had obviously been feasting undisturbed for days.** I got a garden fork, covered my head with a shower hat and poked around in the bin to try and uncover the mystery of the shrinking compost – can a rat really eat that much? My Uncle Ray was visiting (and turned out to be a composting expert – by the way, they're ten a penny) and ordered me to remove all the old grapefruit skins as, he claimed, they would never rot. I put on protective sunglasses and rubber gloves and had a rummage in the muck, but it was a bit like feeling around in the entrails of a decomposing corpse, i.e. completely disgusting. I managed to turn the rotting mess over and, sure enough, there was about six inches of pretty chunky, dark brown material at the bottom, compost in its most basic form – hardly enough to feed a row of lettuces. I had to recover from the experience with a stiff drink and a slice of fruitcake. So, although I will continue to compost, and have built a stone base to deter Mr Rat from returning, let's be honest, I will be purchasing most of my mulch at the bloody garden centre like everyone else, where it comes in large non-eco-friendly plastic bags.

My failure at composting sums up the problem with trying to be green. It can take up a lot of time, and you don't necessarily see any results. **These days, we're made to feel like pariahs if we don't try to do our bit to save the f***ing planet every minute of the day. It's not enough to try and reduce personal debt. It's not enough to help out in the local community. It's not enough to give money to good causes, to say 'hello' to everyone in the street, to smile at hoodies and not moan when the bloke next door is loudly playing utter drivel on his sound system.**

To be able to hold your head up high and be a fully paid-up, responsible member of society in the 21st Century, you have to be seen to be concerned about the environment. Saving the planet has swiftly moved from something people in tepees were obsessed with to a mainstream middle-class objective. **And do you know who the biggest bloody naggers are?** Politicians and pop stars – and they never practise what they preach, do they? I heartily resent being made to feel guilty by Bono and his millionaire mates, many of whom have moved their tax affairs overseas to favourable regimes and who still charter private jets regularly. These days, every newspaper and magazine has to have an ethical living columnist. These self-appointed experts have one mission in life: to make you feel that you're failing at something else by not achieving their targets.

HOW THE MIDDLE CLASSES HIJACKED GREEN ISSUES

The combination of growing environmental awareness and a recession in 2008 meant that the middle classes felt obliged to join the crusade and bombard us with advice and tips stating the f***ing obvious. Everywhere you looked there was yet another lady bountiful lecturing on how to eliminate waste and recycle.

We were told we should return to the wartime frugality of make-do-and-mend, holidaying at home and sensible shopping in order to save the planet.

The government set up the **Energy Saving Trust** and Gordon Brown told us all to eat our greens, stop chucking food in the bin and cut down domestic waste, claiming it cost the average household £8 a week. I don't know where he got that figure, but I do know that in 2007 the government spent the not-inconsiderable sum of £59 million telling us to recycle more. Unfortunately for Gordon, the day after he issued his anti-waste directive, he went to Japan on a specially chartered private jet to attend a G8 summit of world leaders, with the global food crisis top of the agenda. The politicians sat down to a six-course lunch followed by an eight-course dinner.

The government set up WRAP (Waste & Resources Action Programme) to reduce packaging and increase recycling, launching the Love Food Hate Waste campaign. *Cookery writer Rose Prince told us that the clever French had renamed leftovers les restes – and she thought that using old food 'could be sexy'.* Those on a limited budget have always eaten leftovers, but not in the way that these new, middle-class greenies advocate – at one time, we reheated last night's curry in the microwave, ate food past its sell-by date and made the Sunday roast last a week by having cold meat in sandwiches or cooking corned beef hotpot on Tuesdays with sliced up old veg. The fact is, you've got to be pretty middle class to embrace the new mantra of no leftovers and seductive economical cuisine in the first place. You've got to know how to cook creatively, and be able to afford cuts of meat that can be eked out as various dishes over several days. I don't know many working-class families who can afford a large free-range chicken or a whole leg of lamb and who own a mincer. Until the government makes cookery a core subject in all schools, reducing food waste will never catch on. Most people can't cook from scratch, let alone turn a carcass into a rissole with delicious home-made gravy.

I CAN MASTER THE BASICS OF A COUPLE OF LANGUAGES BUT I CAN'T UNDERSTAND GREEN TERMINOLOGY:
SUSTAINABLE
FOOD MILES
CARBON FOOTPRINT
OFFSETTING
LOW IMPACT
NON-TOXIC
CARBON NEUTRAL
POLLUTANT-FREE
ETHICAL

WHY DOES GOING GREEN HAVE TO BE SO COMPLICATED?

According to Which? magazine, the consumer's bible, carbon-offsetting sites, where you donate money to environmental projects to cancel out your carbon emissions (when you travel by air, for example) are *'confusing and inconsistent'*. Frankly, they're just a bit of sticking plaster to make you feel better about that sun-baked fortnight in Thailand.

GREENWASH

UNPICKING THE
TWADDLE

We think it's green to eat seasonal, locally sourced food, but if you live in the UK, how many months of the year are you willing to exist on a diet of potatoes and cabbage? **I naïvely thought that buying imported foods was sinful because of the transport involved. But every food has a carbon footprint – the measure of the impact producing it has on the environment.** Food miles are pretty meaningless, according to top chef Peter Gordon, who says that only 2% of the environmental impact generated by most food from farm to store is down to transport. All along the food chain, from running an office or factory and staffing it (and don't forget all the people who have to travel to work), to planting and harvesting food, to packing and transporting it, a huge amount of carbon emissions is generated.

Put simply, evaluating the eco-credentials of a bunch of roses from Kenya, where they grow in the open air before being put on the plane, or one from the Netherlands, where mostly they are grown in heated greenhouses, is not only complicated, it's totally confusing.

Some supermarkets now label fresh fruit and veg that is flown in by air – but what does that really mean? What about products made closer to home, like sauces and chutneys, which contain ingredients like tamarind, from tropical countries?

Should we stop buying coffee, tea, limes and mangoes, all grown in developing countries which need our business to support their economy?

Globally, extreme weather like droughts and floods means we will always have to import food – it's a myth to think otherwise. Trade is crucial to the world's economy, and as long as you are happy with the conditions and pay of the workers who grow the food you purchase, what's the problem? At the end of the day, you might find that migrant workers living and working in the UK picking strawberries and cockles live in worse conditions than those harvesting Marks & Spencer's peas in Africa.

In the end, food and drink accounts for only 5% of the average person's carbon footprint (19% is transport and 9% is produced by power used at home), so if you feel like eating a papaya, go right ahead.

Walk around Britain's lavish temple to ethically sourced food, Whole Foods in Kensington, West London, and what do you see? Couples staggering out with their bags, loading them into gas-guzzling 4x4s, and then driving off to their country retreats. Going green seems to be an elastic concept as far as the middle classes are concerned.

The most depressing piece of green propaganda I've read recently was about an 'eco-diet' devised by scientists at Cardiff University, which analysed the ecological footprint from farm to plate of everything you might want to eat. Unpackaged, locally grown vegetables were OK, but not wine, spirits, chocolate, ice-cream and most meat, because breeding livestock uses up a lot of energy. Cheese is evil too, because of the amount of energy required to process and store it.

Frankly, life's too short to spend it chewing on a stick of celery or eating carrots.

Farmers claim that if we all became full-time vegetarians it would have little impact on the environment in the UK, because agriculture accounts for just 1% of our CO_2 emissions. I'm happier having meat-free Mondays – you certainly feel better. *As for the amount of methane produced by cattle, that has fallen by 14% over the last twenty years and could be brought down further if their diet was changed their and manure used to produce bio-fuels.* If pastures were turned over to growing corn and grain, the countryside would be altered forever and it wouldn't have much impact on the world's food supply. The arguments about green food production are complex, with hype and hysteria on both sides.

IS SHOPPING SINFUL IN OUR NEW GREEN WORLD?

There's a group of fanatical greenies arguing that our rampant consumerism is destroying the planet. We buy stuff we don't need, and chuck away more than we should, adding to landfill waste which causes the rise in greenhouse gasses. The counter-argument runs that trade and consumerism oil the world economy and get money spread out around the globe to people who would otherwise be living in poverty. Interestingly, the amount of our household budget we spend on food has actually gone down – it was 16% in 1987 and had dropped to 9% twenty years later. When the full impact of the recession hit, people economised on food, and sales of organic produce, which had risen by 1000% over a decade, plummeted by 20% in six months in 2008. Meanwhile, sales of in-house brands soared, as did the takings of the cheaper supermarket chains like Aldi, Netto and Lidl.

It seemed that being green was a designer option – when the shit hit the fan, financially speaking, we didn't care where the f***ing bacon had come from or whether those chickens were knee-deep in their own shit. We wanted to eat for less and pay the mortgage.

Sales of takeaway pizzas boomed, and you can't tell me that they are eco-friendly. Food prices rose at a disproportionate rate as countries like China switched to eating wheat. Poor harvests, higher energy and fuel costs didn't help. Our confusion about consumerism extended to fashion. Even though documentaries and high-profile charity campaigns highlighted the often appalling conditions endured by workers producing cheap fashion for high-street chains, after an initial dip in profits at the start of the recession, many retailer reported sales had risen again.

With less money to spend, we still preferred to buy disposable fashion as a way of lifting our spirits amidst all the talk of financial meltdown.

It's all very well for fashion editors to talk about buying 'key' pieces that will last for many seasons, but the truth is, most women don't think like that and never will. They treat fashion as a harmless drug, perfectly acceptable when you need cheering up, and who can blame them? When even Michelle Obama is wearing colourful clothes from the downmarket US chain J. Crew, the message is clear – cheap is OK.

SPARE ME THESE SUPERMARKET SAINTS

Greenwash is the perfect way to describe the long rinse cycle of fresh initiatives that retailers unveil every week, claiming they will help avert ecological disaster. Britain's most successful supermarket chain, Tesco, gave £25 million to Manchester University to fund the Sustainable Consumption Institute. The notion that a company whose stated aim is total domination of the retail market is planning to invest in research in 'sustainable consumption' is risible. **It's like giving the Vatican a grant to research new forms of birth control.**

Supermarkets are about increasing consumption, not reducing it, delivering maximum profits to their shareholders in the process. It's as simple as that.

Most new superstores are sited on the edge of towns, away from most public transport and generally accessible only by car. They are surrounded by acres of parking – few stores ever build it underneath or on top of the shop. Supermarkets have single-handedly concreted over vast swathes of the countryside, all in the name of retail. *When I visited a local superstore recently, the lights were blazing and almost every shopper was taking handfuls of plastic bags.* Tesco has started a two-year trial of labelling carbon footprints (in association with the Carbon Trust) on twenty products across four ranges – orange juice, detergents, light bulbs and potatoes – which shows how many grams of carbon dioxide have been used to produce a single serving.

Judging by the size of the backsides on the majority of shoppers I saw, quite a few sacks of potatoes constitute an 'average serving', so the new labelling could be virtually useless.

Educating us in how to protect the environment will not be achieved by confusing initiatives like this – a classic case of greenwash. The Carbon Trust has the cheek to tell us how to cook potatoes in order to minimise carbon emissions – it seems that baking them in the oven is worse than bunging them in the microwave.

GREENWASH

Call me a major polluter, but I will never give a nasty microwave space in my kitchen. As we import half our vegetables and 95% of our fruit, the best thing to do is buy local, and you're then entitled to cook your veg exactly how you like.

Marks & Spencer, meanwhile, ploughs ahead with its £200 million environmentally conscious Plan A – amongst other measures, its wares will be delivered in new articulated trailers carrying 16% more stuff and using 10% less fuel. They held a coat-hanger 'amnesty' recently, when you could take back any unwanted plastic hangers. That should let you sleep easier for a few nights.

Unfortunately, Plan A is not really joined-up thinking. If you buy lunch at M&S they still hand out dozens of small plastic bags to every person buying a sandwich, which is already in a packet. A mountain of plastic cutlery is stacked by the tills to enable you to consume your overpriced, overpackaged little pots of jumbo couscous and bean salad. Plan A doesn't seem to have covered the possibility of giving out biodegradable card utensils. OK, M&S now produces key clothing ranges in Fairtrade cotton, as well as polyester schoolwear made from recycled bottles, but they're in business to get us to purchase as much as possible, not recycle last year's coat and skirt.

Plan A, ultimately, is window-dressing and, in the harsh world of retail, M&S need to ensure that their profits remain healthy.

Now the battle for our green pounds has moved to garden centres, and Wyevale, the UK's largest chain, is going to convert its stores into 'green' shopping malls targeted at the over-60s baby-boomers. Plans include building 'environmentally friendly' stores in these malls for third-party retailers. **How does building a mall where there wasn't one before help the environment? In spite of their new green credentials, I doubt we'll see any retailers sign up to 'buy nothing day' or 'lights out for an hour' – both grass-roots initiatives which have swept around the world.** When you hear that McDonald's is running a fleet of lorries powered on recycled cooking oil from its outlets, and B&Q claims it can make our homes more energy-efficient (but still stocks plastic garden furniture and patio heaters), you don't really take them seriously. *Retailers have seized on the notion of protecting the environment as a way of driving sales, and they've been very successful – household spending on 'ethical' goods and services has almost doubled over the past five years.*

WASTE NOT WANT NOT?

I try to do my bit when it comes to recycling. **I religiously refuse plastic carriers, cramming meat and veg into cloth bags better suited to a couple of books.** I wash out yoghurt and cream containers. **I collect bottles, taking them to recycling bins at night so that the neighbours can't see how much is being drunk at my house.** I stagger to the dump with unwanted gadgets, the old car battery, that blender that doesn't work. I actually save string!

But somehow, no matter how hard I might try, I end up with a pile of waste sitting by the road waiting for someone else to deal with. Last year millions of shoppers dumped plastic carrier bags – well done! The braver amongst us took the next step and started leaving packaging behind at the checkout. We went along with our council's complicated recycling

schemes, sorting rubbish into different categories, reading the calendars they sent us listing what waste would be collected on which day for the year ahead. We squashed squash bottles, folded up papers and envelopes and crammed them into clear plastic bags. We made sure our weeds fitted into green garden waste bags we'd been ordered to purchase. **In short, we felt quite virtuous, because we'd tried to be environmentally aware in our own small way.** And what happened?

In short, we were too good at being green. Ten years ago, the amount of household rubbish designated recyclable in the UK was less than 10%; now it's risen to a third. *But only half of all the paper saved is processed in Britain. Same with glass and plastic, which is sent to countries such as China to be recycled.* Shipping rubbish around the globe doesn't sound that green, does it? The answer would be for us to use our rubbish for local energy-generating schemes, which countries such as Denmark are very good at. Unfortunately, no one wants giant chimneys and incinerators in their backyards. If local people could be involved in designing and deciding where they were built, it could work.

Retailers must cut down on packaging, and we have to stop being Nimbys and accept that the only way to deal with rubbish long-term is closer to home.

Once upon a time, back in the dim and distant 1980s, how we yearned to be middle class! No one wanted to be saddled with the stigma of being considered part of the common working class – after all, our mums and dads had strived all their lives to move up the social scale away from their humble roots, and we were ruthlessly determined to better ourselves, too. By the 1980s more people than ever before had managed to buy their own homes, even though it would mean a lifetime of debt and a fundamental change in how we managed our personal finances. From now on, life would be on tick, and debt was no longer seen as socially unacceptable by working men and women. We all had it. In the 1950s, people only bought what they could afford, but thirty years later, consumerism was well and truly booming. The idea of 'need' had been completely subverted – to my generation, 'need' was whatever you wanted, bought with a credit card, and why not?

I saw this fundamental change at first hand, starting my life in half a terraced house in an inner-city street, being allowed to use the bathroom once a week, with an outside toilet in the backyard, with a mother who would cross London for a bargain, who carefully hoarded coupons for discounts, and who fed and clothed the family on a very limited budget. Dad grew vegetables on the family allotment, and all holidays were taken in the UK, in whatever second-hand car he'd managed to graduate to that year. The shame of driving down to Cornwall in a vehicle that had been used as a hearse! *I didn't eat in a restaurant till I was sixteen – and then only as a reward for passing exams at school.* We ate picnics on our outings, brewed up tea on a

primus stove, ate sand-encrusted sandwiches on windy beaches and in noisy lay-bys when we went blackberry picking each autumn. Marmalade was

auntie Vi, mum, Ray & uncle Ray & sister Pat Anglesey 1954 x

bought in massive discount tins and spooned into small pots for the breakfast table. **<u>Christmas turkeys were bought on Christmas Eve, as the street markets were closing and there were bargains to be had.</u>** I was born just after rationing ended, but that mentality lasted right through my formative years.

The need to economise and make do during the Second World War shaped our parents' whole attitude to life.

They weren't the kind of people who would waste money on unnecessary luxuries, but were savers who bought Premium Bonds and felt uncomfortable with debt. Their parents had instilled in them the need to be self-sufficient at all costs, especially at a time of rationing and food shortages. Like most of their friends and relatives, my parents came from humble backgrounds, often sharing rented houses with other family members, and so it was important to buy a house – no matter how small – of their own. Having left school at fourteen with no qualifications, they were obsessed with self-improvement: Dad studied at evening classes and became an electrical engineer; Mum lied about her schooling to get a cushy job in the civil service. If they were alive today, they'd have no problem with the current recession … coping with financial constraints was second nature to their generation. **Mum saw nothing demeaning about housework, in spite of having a full-time job. Dad spent every**

hour, when not working or studying, tending to his allotment. He turned the garage into an electrical repair shop, tinkering with old televisions and radios, bringing them back to life and selling them to the neighbours. Our hi-fi was a museum piece, in full working order.

In short, they were never happier than when they were busy saving money.

Dad would redecorate the house every few years, hanging up wallpaper, painting skirting boards and ceilings, plastering over any cracks. Forget about taking the car to be serviced – he'd do it himself, as well as repaving the bit of driveway where his pride and joy sat when not in use. He could repair leaky taps and plumb in a new bath, rebuild kitchen cupboards and fix broken chairs. Mum and Dad's generation were the original DIYers; in fact, one of the

THE CASTE SYSTEM

only bits of reading material in our home (apart from a set of encyclopaedias, the Bible and the collected works of Daphne du Maurier) was several years' worth of Practical Householder magazine, lovingly stowed in date order. Every winter Mum or Auntie Vi would knit me a horrible cardigan with big plastic buttons down the front (emphasising my flat chest), which I did my best to lose or pull into a more flattering baggy shape.

Naturally, I (and most of my friends) reacted strongly against all this intensive nest-building. On leaving school, we couldn't wait to stop scrimping and start shagging.

We'd had 'waste not, want not' shoved down our throats from birth and had been ordered to eat everything on our plates at every meal. I did learn to sew (because I couldn't afford to buy clothes and, anyway, my taste was too outlandish for any shops in our area), eventually cadging mum's sewing machine, but only in order to run up avant-garde outfits for my clubbing activities – Bermuda shorts and skimpy op art shift dresses, raincoats made from silver leather and striped PVC trousers. I'd sail

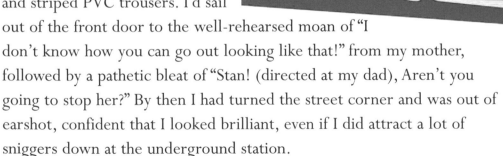

out of the front door to the well-rehearsed moan of "I don't know how you can go out looking like that!" from my mother, followed by a pathetic bleat of "Stan! (directed at my dad), Aren't you going to stop her?" By then I had turned the street corner and was out of earshot, confident that I looked brilliant, even if I did attract a lot of sniggers down at the underground station.

The minute I rented my first flat I employed a cleaning lady.

Housework was a thing of the past in my world, even though I was earning a tiny salary as a writer on a teenage magazine. *I'd spent years before I left home doing the ironing every Sunday morning in order to qualify for a pitiful amount of pocket money and I swore I would never do it again!* Although I eventually learned to cook in my mid-twenties (I only did one term of cookery at school before studying Latin and Spanish), like most of my friends I had no intention of mending anything.

My generation grew up getting someone else to do all the things we couldn't face: wiping up after the kids, cleaning the house, mending our cars, fixing washing machines and weeding the garden. At the same time we formed our social networks around shared interests: friends from work, people in our income bracket.

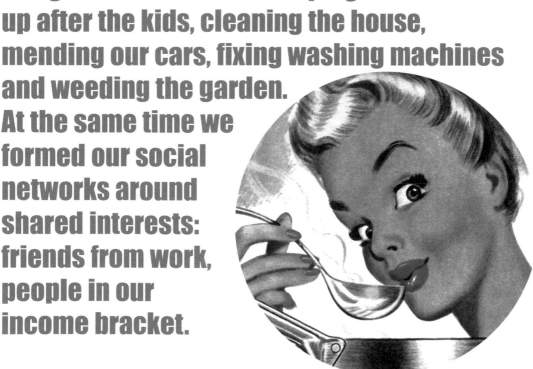

THE CASTE SYSTEM

Credit cards allowed us to purchase our dreams instantly, and postpone facing up to the economic reality of whether we could afford the lifestyles we were enjoying. The old class system was evolving, but didn't disappear – the new middle class was so big (everyone had joined it except the very old, the very young and the very poor) we had to subdivide it up according to where we lived. Before, posh people lived in selected bits of London, in period houses in cities like Bath and Edinburgh, or in large houses in the countryside. Their children attended boarding schools. **By the 1990s, oiks (the nouveau posh) could afford private schools, flashy cars and designer clothes.** Led by property developers, pop stars and television personalities, they invaded the countryside and bought big houses, then started playing at being farmers, keeping horses, designer chickens and ducks. They made cheese, sold their own jam, and even created their own rare-breed sausages.

The old pecking order with the aristos at one end and manual workers at the other was totally irrelevant by the end of the 20th Century. Immigrants were the worker bees, keeping everybody's lives functioning and their homes clean and tidy.

The recession has affected everyone – but has it really changed our class system? All the evidence is that it hasn't – the snobbery and the subtle demarcation lines that mark out old and new money still prevail. But with disposable income dropping by more than £150 a month, suddenly all those much-maligned skills our mums had in abundance don't seem so useless any more. For the last year, you haven't been able to open a newspaper or a magazine without some smug recessionista telling you how to make a rissole, soak beans or turn unwanted T-shirts into the latest fashion, boasting about how she shopped at supermarkets like the once-considered-naff Netto or Lidl for bargain lobsters and cheap olive oil. One major drawback with a lot of this new advice, like telling us to comb the Internet for bargains, is that it takes up a lot of the one commodity many of us don't have – time. Let's be brutally honest here – does anyone really know (or want to know) how to sew a frock from scratch? Plant potatoes so they actually produce more spuds and don't get eaten by slugs? Put up a shelf and assemble something from IKEA?

We may lack these practical skills, but we've arrived in the 21st Century world-beaters at one thing: personal debt!

We've got massive mortgages on homes we can't sell, even if we tried. Wallets full of credit cards with bills we can't pay off, incurring crippling interest each month. We want our kids to succeed, so many of us sent them to private schools and nurseries with exorbitant fees. We've bought trendy cars that guzzle fuel, and who knows whether we can afford to switch on the central heating in winter?

How to cope?

Annoyingly, a band of new experts has sprung up telling us **HOW TO SHAPE UP AND BE POSITIVE. ACCORDING TO THEM, WE'VE GOT THE CHANCE TO JOIN A NEW CASTE – THE FRUGALISTAS, PEOPLE WHO ARE GOING TO COPE MAGNIFICENTLY,** who will rise to the challenge, just as our parents and grandparents did. *What's fascinating about these pundits is how posh they are.* It's all a bit Marie Antoinette, dishing out advice you personally are never likely to take. Take blonde, bubbly Celia Walden, a columnist on The Daily Telegraph and girlfriend of former newspaper editor and telly star Piers Morgan. Celia's family used to live in a grand house in Kensington (which Piers has now bought), and she specialises in writing features about the rich and famous, regularly managing to get herself in the photographs.

One of her trademark pieces recently was entitled 'Darling, Money is so Last Year'. She claimed 'being rich can be such a bore. Choice … is taken away when you can have it all.'

And she quotes Peter York, who co-authored *The Official Sloane Ranger Handbook*, as saying 'humble and threadbare is what the English do best. This recession has given us a lovely excuse to behave in a way that comes quite naturally to us … Now there is a delight in rediscovering poverty.'

Of course, if you are struggling to stop your house being repossessed and have been laid off or asked to work part-time, this kind of irony (I'm being kind here) isn't even remotely entertaining.

These frugalistas specialise in the sweeping statement — according to Celia Walden, 'as the country unites in Blitz spirit … [the new faux poor] tell lies about being forced to downsize their houses, bonuses and expense accounts while exaggerating the amount of money they've lost'. They even, it seems, boast about using public transport — how very daring! It is true that expensive restaurants seem packed, with quite a few people pretending they're economising by eating two starters instead of a main course, but is that really a true barometer of how the recession is affecting society overall? **LET'S PLAY AT BEING POOR** is the game the well-bred and upper-middle class have taken to like ducks to water. **Vogue magazine proudly brought back their More Dash Than Cash feature, tying bits of Liberty fabric to cheap shoes and featuring high street T-shirts alongside expensive shirts, telling you how to make a simple Chanel dress work for day into evening. They still use exactly the same models – thin, glamorous and certainly not poor.**

The people who are doing well out of the recession are supermarkets (selling more fresh food as the trend for eating at home continues) and kitchen suppliers. The preoccupation with thrift has become big business – a spokeswoman from Lakeland said, 'When everyone is worried about money, it's lovely to return to home values'. One of their preserving pans costs £39 – but the company call it a 'life-time purchase'.

Of course you could be like me and make jam, pasta, chilli con carne for parties, baked beans and Irish stew in exactly the same pot, which cost about £12 from my local hardware store.

The whacky economics that dictate you will make jam and preserves to save money, but first you'll have to spend £40 on gadgets, is so FAUX POOR. That's a lot of jam before break-even point.

The publishing world has been quick to capitalise on the downturn – Penguin Books brought out **Keeping Poultry and Rabbits on Scraps**, which originally appeared in 1941, written to help people coping with food shortages during the war. A company spokesman said, 'It's great to see those tried-and-tested methods being used again'.

OF COURSE THEY HAVE TO SAY THAT – THEY ARE FLOGGING THE BOOK.

Mark my words, this little volume of retro-chic is being purchased as a bedtime book, a joke gift, and for people who wouldn't know a Rhode Island Red from a cocktail. People in flats, city dwellers, people who live miles from work, aren't going to be rushing home from work to tend f***ing chickens and feed them leftovers. IF THEY ARE THAT POOR THEY WILL HAVE TURNED THE BLOODY LEFTOVERS FROM SUPPER INTO THE NEXT DAY'S PACKED LUNCH, NEVER MIND THE SODDING CHICKENS!

THE CASTE SYSTEM

And if you are truly broke, would you be tempted to buy a book called *The Thrifty Cookbook: 476 Ways to Eat Well with Left-overs*, what your wartime granny could teach you about diet, thrift and going green? **A new kind of cuisine – eco-cookery – has been spawned, which incorporates the new mantras of economy and saving the planet.** One self-appointed expert is Sheherazade Goldsmith, whose husband Zac is a well-known environmental campaigner. He's also the heir to his financier father's billions, and a Tory parliamentary candidate. Sheherazade, described as a former model and environmentalist, writes a magazine column called Green Scene, and I am indebted to her for the following top tip:

> DID YOU KNOW THAT PUTTING A LID ON A PAN WHILE YOU'RE COOKING ... CAN CUT COOKING TIME BY 75%? thus saving energy.

IMAGINE – SHE ACTUALLY EARNED MONEY WRITING THAT!!! Sadly, our wealthy eco-cook goes on to recommend an £88 casserole and a £39 frying pan so, clearly, there's not a lot of economy living going on in her Elizabethan farmhouse. In another magazine she swears by £17 hand cream, and waxes lyrical about the cottage pie from the most fashionable (and expensive) butcher in West London, Lidgates of Holland Park. **IF SHE'S SO BLOODY GREEN, HOW COME THIS SILLY COW ISN'T MAKING HER OWN COTTAGE PIE? IT'S DEAD EASY.** Buying your meat at Lidgates is like choosing Harrods for your toilet rolls – a sign you are a bit of a label queen.

Since the recession, newspapers and magazines have searched for glamorous new women they could dub frugalistas and make the rest of us feel we were failing at something else. We were asked to believe these women did a full day's work in the office and then dashed home to change into old clothes to kill slugs. They proudly

announced they'd cut up their credit cards, banned foreign holidays and had started swapping home-made soup recipes with friends.

There seemed to be a competition running in Middle England to see who could economise the most. These demented harpies trawled for sawmills where they could buy off-cuts for their wood-burning stoves, and boasted that they did their washing at night when the electricity was cheaper. They held 'swap and slurp' nights where they drank cheap wine and swapped unwanted clothes. It was described as 'a chance to explore their inner domestic goddesses'.

PASS THE SICK BAG.

GIRLS' FRIENDLY SOCIETY
CERTIFICATE

I don't know what's been worse over the last couple of years: the Marie Antoinettes in the posh newspapers or the middle-class women competing to be the Queens of Thrift.

> ## Next, they'll be telling us they only wash once a week and turn their knickers inside out every other day.

I am sure that there has been an increase in people wanting to learn new skills – from practical ones like sewing and knitting to foreign languages or IT skills that may help them get a job. But most of the information we are fed is actually supplied by people with a vested interest. What I feel sure of is that for every ten who start a self-improvement course, more than half will drop out.

THE CASTE SYSTEM

If anything, the recession has reinforced the class divide.

If you were poor at the start, you've got less. If you were rich – well, you might have less now, but your less is a darn sight more than most people have.

Research has shown categorically that the British class system is more rigid than almost any other country, certainly America and most of Europe. In spite of more than a decade of Labour government, the gap between rich and poor remains exactly the same. The recession has seen the class system morph into the caste system – you largely stay within the band you were born into. Pretending that debt has somehow thrown us all into the same social mix is patently untrue. **The sons and daughters of famous or successful people still do better (on average) than children from low-income families.** *If your dad is a politician, a newspaper editor, a film producer or a*

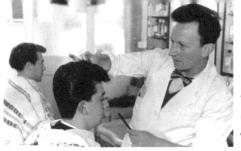

lawyer, then you've got a better chance in life. That hasn't changed in fifty years. When I consider my own background, it's a miracle that I got where I have in class-ridden Britain. All that's new is that the frugalistas have told us that collecting and using discount coupons is chic. (In my mother's day it was ration coupons.) **We are told to loathe consumers and love conservers, but deep down, we're born to buy, aren't we? How can you re-programme an entire generation of shoppers?** What has boomed is new ways of social networking via the recession – swapping, knitting, seed swaps, community kitchens, car pooling and bartering services. **Maybe we will start talking to our neighbours rather than via the Internet – but I doubt it.**

Yes, let's turn off the lights, put those pesky lids on our pans and grow lettuce on our windowsills, but please can we stop trying to turn the clock back to a Golden Age of Austerity? You need a world war for that.

Auntie POP & mum in our back garden

CONCLUSION

So here we are at the end of our journey. I'll tell you what I've learned from writing this book — you have to wade through mountains of unnecessary advice, useless tips and unimportant 'objectives' to realise one basic fact: you have to be in control. You need to wrestle it back from the nanny state, from interfering bureaucrats and from well-meaning but nosy neighbours and relatives.

I read a letter in the newspaper recently that summed up a lot of the twaddle we encounter each day:

'We live in wonderful times ... someone has discovered how to eliminate all problems. This has been achieved by replacing the word 'problem' with the word 'issue'. Every day one hears talk of someone having health issues, marital issues and so forth.' Exactly.

Have you noticed, too, how people are obsessed with achieving happiness? It's become a new sport like cycling or hurdling, something you have to learn. Something else you can fail at, or not make the grade. A government advisor on green issues has actually suggested we should have happiness lessons, and a Campaign For Happiness has been launched via the website TopTips.com. Unfortunately, the founder of this campaign revealed that she'd sought advice from Alain de Botton, author of the best-selling books *The Architecture of Happiness* and *The Consolations of Philosophy*. When his most recent effort, *The Pleasures and Sorrows of Work*, received a bum review in the USA, here's what this guru of happiness emailed the critic in question:

'I WILL HATE YOU TILL THE DAY I DIE.'
NOT A LOT OF HAPPINESS-SPREADING EVIDENT THERE...

Which only goes to show how wonderfully inconsistent so-called experts are when it comes to their own lives. I've always had a shit list of people who were mean about me, mocked my teeth, my glasses and my accent. I rejoice when their careers falter, they get sacked or split up with their partners. Alain, welcome to my club – it's called Divine Retribution.

Don't get overwhelmed by outside forces. Even if you make a decision that proves to be a bit of a mistake, it's not the end of the world. The Czech writer Milan Kundera wrote a novel entitled *The Unbearable Lightness of Being*. It was a reaction against Nietzsche's theory that every event in the world will 'eternally return', i.e. happen again. Kundera says you've got one life to lead and nothing repeats itself. 'Lightness' means that decisions and events aren't that important.

Lightness is also not accumulating too much stuff to worry about.
       Too many possessions.
 Too many handbags, cars, frocks, and potted plants.
In the end, friends are your most valued possessions. The state and bureaucracy are something to be kept in check and not allowed to dominate your precious time.

Lightness means removing these unnecessary weights from your shoulders.

Instead of trying to run the world, take control of your back garden, your neighbourhood and your local high street. Don't set goals you'll fail at.

Being positive is empowering. FIGHT BACK!

USEFUL ADDRESSES, FURTHER READING, ADVICE ETC.

MUMBO JUMBO

Further information

senseaboutscience.org.uk
Charity devoted to debunking myths and cutting through the claptrap about science. Downloadable leaflets from their website.
The Truth About Stress by Angela Patmore, Atlantic Books.

SHOPPING

See also Money and The New Etiquette.

fixtureferrets.co.uk
A pay-to-join website that finds the best supermarket promotions for groceries.

moneymagpie.com
As well as featuring the best deals for saving and borrowing, there are hints on bargain shopping.

myvouchercodes.co.uk
Plenty of discounts for your online purchases.

uk.freecycle.org
Website matches people who have things they no longer want with people who can use them. Sign up to find your local group.

GROW YOUR OWN

Allotments and garden sharing

allotment.org.uk
Claims to be the most popular allotment website in the UK. Interesting topics and plenty of advice.

eatseasonably.co.uk
Advice on when fruit and veg are at their seasonal best.

gardenlend.co.uk
Links neglected gardens with keen gardeners who have nowhere to garden.

grofun.org.uk
Growing Real Organic Food in Urban Neighbourhoods is a scheme based in Bristol, but could be easily replicated anywhere, bringing locals together to share knowledge and tools for growing food in their back gardens.

growingcommunities.org
Social enterprise in Hackney, East London. Runs an Organic Box Scheme and a Good Food Swap at Christmas, where everything is made, grown, picked or found. Mince pies traded for oyster mushrooms – sounds like a good idea worth copying.

guerillagardening.org
Encourages you to make over neglected public spaces, so if you don't have a garden it's a way of achieving a share in one. Gives advice on how to get started plotting and planting, creating your own 'cell'.

landshare.channel4.com
Connects growers with landowners.

nationaltrust.org
For details of their allotment schemes.

nsalg.org.uk
The website of the National Society of Allotment and Leisure Gardeners. Good links, especially the Plants Reunited online plant swap.

Blogs

guardian.co.uk/gardening-blog
independent.co.uk/emmatownshend
Seasonally appropriate gardening tips.

General advice

eatseasonably.co.uk
Good advice on what to grow and when.

railwaysleeper.com
Great website with loads of examples of projects using recycled railway sleepers, telegraph poles, beams and oak barrels – good

for making raised beds to grow veg and landscape your garden. Will deliver anywhere in the UK.

rhs.org.uk

The Royal Horticultural Society's website will answer loads of your queries and also publishes a downloadable leaflet about composting. The My Garden forum is where gardeners exchange tips, offer advice and share seeds – it's very good. If you join the RHS, you can apply for up to 20 packets of seeds from 700 varieties harvested from RHS gardens like Wisley, Harlow Carr and Hyde Hall.

Seeds and plants

Local markets

I buy vegetable plants from stalls at weekly markets in my area (North Yorkshire). Then you know they are suited to your climate and, at about a £1 a bundle, they're great value.

mammothonion.co.uk

The website of vegetable specialist Robinsons of Preston (it supplies onion and leek seeds for exhibition growers, but the cabbages and Brussels sprouts are also good). If you live in the North you can visit the nursery to talk vegetables.

plantswap.co.uk
seedypeople.co.uk

Seed- and plant-swapping forums.

realseeds.co.uk

Nice website and interesting seeds, complete with sowing guides. The owners really know their products and money isn't wasted on fancy packaging. They also tell you how to collect seeds from your own plants.

THE NEW YOU

See The Caste System.

THE NEW ETIQUETTE

See also Money and Shopping.

Cheap clothing

be-a-fashionista.com

Designer bags to rent – much cheaper than buying one!

bigwardrobe.com

Fashionable clothes that can be swapped or sold.

eBay.co.uk

Huge online marketplace for just about everything.

swishing.co.uk

Clothes swapping for women.

swishing.org

The site explains swishing and how it works, and encourages you to 'switch and ditch' with a group of friends. They bring along clothes and accessories they want to swap, you explain the 'rules of the rail' and then everything is up for grabs.

whatsmineisyours.com

Site for swapping clothes and furniture. Small list of online boutiques.

MONEY

Cheap books

bookfinder4u.com
comparebookprices.co.uk

Both sites offer a free service to find the best book prices.

bookmooch.com.

To get books, you need to give books away. An international site.

readitswapit.co.uk

Over 180,000 books listed on this swap club.

Cosmetics online

eyeslipsface.co.uk
sallyexpress.com
strawberrynet.com

Bargains to be had on these websites, especially if you buy in bulk.

Energy-saving

energysavingtrust.org.uk; tel 0800 512 012

Free impartial advice on saving money and fighting climate change.

warmfront.co.uk; tel 0800 316 2805

Government-funded initiative to make homes more energy-efficient by providing a package of insulation and heating improvements. Check if you qualify for a grant or rebate.

General advice

adviceguide.org.uk
Free online advice on benefits, employment, bankruptcy and debt management from the Citizens Advice Bureau. Will locate your local bureau.

confused.com
Helps you find the best insurance, mortgage and money deals. Also explains how to switch utility suppliers.

moneysavingexpert.com
Martin Lewis' website gives good general advice, as well as tips on freebies, saving money on utilities, mortgages and the like.

nationaldebtline.co.uk; tel: 0808 808 4000
Free confidential and independent advice to help you deal with debts.

tuc.org.uk
Has a downloadable leaflet called Coping with the Economic Downturn, a practical guide for working people and their families. It tells you about redundancy, benefits you can claim, how to deal with debt, looking for a new job, and getting training.

Mobile phones and reducing your phone bills

grumbletext.co.uk
Consumer complaints and action site. Tells you how to fight premium rate scams.

environfone.com
mobile2cash.co.uk
mobilephonebuyer.net
All these sites offer cash for old mobiles.

saynoto0870.com
How to reduce call costs to some numbers by looking up alternative providers.

Selling and swapping

flogit4u.com
i-sold4u.com
serialsellers.com
stuffusell.com
These companies sell your stuff online and take a commission.

swapz.co.uk
The biggest direct-swap website. Free to join.

GREENWASH

Local exchanges

letslinkuk.net
LETS stands for Local Exchange Trading Schemes and has appeared in a storyline in The Archers! A community-based system of mutual aid, open to all ages and abilities. Members see it as a way of eventually replacing money: do something for someone from your local group and gain points to trade with another member. Now has a worldwide network.

timebanking.org
Time banking is described as a way of strengthening the non-market economy by focussing on social support, from DIY to childcare, driving, trips out, exercise, making new friends, learning new skills and crafts. Members 'deposit' their time by offering practical help to others and 'withdraw' their time when they need something done themselves. Everyone's time is valued equally.

Local food

farma.org.uk
Represents farm shops and producers who do home deliveries. Easy-to-use map of regional providers.

farmersmarkets.net
Directory of Farmers' Markets in the UK, with good links to a wide range of organisations that promote British produce, agriculture, rural and consumer issues.

Recycling and waste management

communitycompost.org
Local communities organise to manage their waste.

recyclenow.com
A government-funded website that encourages us to recycle. PET symbols explained and compost bins at subsidised prices. Easy step-by-step guide to composting.

uk.freecycle.org.
Over one million members in more than 450 groups in the UK. Easy to find your local group on the site, then subscribe and start posting the items you want to get rid of.

THE CASTE SYSTEM

General advice

direct.gov.uk
The official government website with links to local councils. Categories include Health and well-being, Money, Citizens and rights, Justice and the law. People categories as well, which are surprisingly detailed and with some nuggets of information that aren't in government-speak. Other areas of interest include how to start a community group, waste and recycling, car pooling and how to balance your carbon emissions.

Joining new clubs

gumtree.com
meetup.com
The places to look to find clubs for every sort of interest, from book and writing clubs to chocolate-tasting, photography to 80s music.

Knitting

castoff.info
The UK's largest club for beginners and experienced knitters with over 50 venues. Good home page and chatroom.

Knit it!
Let's Knit!
Simply Knitting
Source local groups from the classified ads in these magazines.

knitchicks.co.uk.
The website for hip knitting communities. Features include 'Knitting on planes'.

knittaplease.com
Avant-garde site with everything from knitting graffiti to knitted sauce bottle covers!

laughinghens.com
Online heaven for knitting and crochet devotees who want to find the best wool, patterns and workshops.

stitchnbitch.co.uk.
Global knitting and crocheting club. Tells you how to set up a group in your area.

Selling (and buying) hand-made things

etsy.com
Operates a bit like eBay – they take a fee for selling your goods.

Sew your own clothes

fitzpatterns.com.
Downloadable patterns for the younger market.

freeneedle.com.
Compiled by Miss Stitch and the gang, a directory of free information about sewing and needlecrafts on the Internet. Easy to search for a specific pattern.

knitandsew.co.uk
Linked to Learn to Knit magazine. Claims to be the UK's largest haberdashery shop. Huge number of categories.

printsew.com
Pick a pattern, click on it, print it and sew it. Wide choice of design ranges.

reprodepot.com
Vintage repro and retro fabrics, with some fabulous designs and patterns. Small but good selection of buttons etc.

sewessential.co.uk
Haberdashery and sewing supplies.

sewing.org.
Good range of free patterns and, if you want to know how to make a skirt from an old pair of jeans, this is a good site.

Picture Credits

Page 57: Images International
Page 90: www.bigpicturesphoto.com